My Culinary Journey

FOOD and FÊTES of PROVENCE

with recipes

by Georgeanne Brennan

yellow pear press

Narrative portion originally published in *A Pig in Provence* by Georgeanne Brennan and reprinted with permission from Chronicle Books.

ISBN 978-0-9970664-0-1

Manufactured in Hong Kong.

Designed by Rose Wright.
Cover food styling by Bruce Wright.

Published by Yellow Pear Press, LLC.
www.yellowpearpress.com

10 9 8 7 6 5 4 3 2 1

Distributed by Publishers Group West.

In memory of
Donald Brennan
1936 – 2014

When my memoir, *A Pig in Provence*, on which *My Culinary Journey* is based, was published, readers wrote to me, asking for more recipes and for photos. In *My Culinary Journey*, I've been able to pack the pages with some of my favorite recipes, many of which I first cooked in Provence, and to offer photos to bring to life the landscape, markets, and kitchens of that luminous region of France.

As you'll discover in the narrative of this book, my husband and I bought a farmhouse in Provence in 1970 and moved there with our toddler daughter shortly thereafter to live a rural life raising goats and pigs and making cheese. We acted on a vision, and I discovered not only a way of life but also a way of thinking about life, food, and the land that was to stay with me and to form the basis of a culinary career of writing and teaching about food. Although I've written award-winning cooking books as well as gardening books, my heart still belongs to the simple rhythms of the land and the seasons.

These rhythms are celebrated every day in the markets and kitchens of Provence, but on a grander scale, even an historical scale, they are also celebrated in Provence's numerous village festivals and fêtes. You'll find fêtes of all kinds extolling the virtues of the land and sea. There are fêtes celebrating lavender, wheat, olives, linden leaves, sardines, and even sea urchins. Festivals are held around events such as the transhumance, when herds of sheep are moved from the valleys to the mountains in summer along ancient trails, then back again in winter. Gypsies come from all over Europe to the Camargue for a festival centered around their patron saint, Sarah. Community feasts are frequently a key element in the fêtes and festivals, where meals are prepared for hundreds of people focusing on a special dish, such as a grand aïoli with loads of the garlicky mayonnaise served with vegetables and fish, or a grand bouillabaisse where competing groups vie to make the best.

Anyone can participate in these meals, but tickets must be purchased early. The fêtes and festivals are advertised well beforehand with flyers posted in and around the villages, and today, they are also announced on internet sites of the villages, and departments of tourism. These fêtes, like the markets and the food of Provence, remain authentic, and I've tried here, with words, photos and recipes, to bring the inimitable Provençal passion for food and celebration into clear focus.

A Personal History
of Goat Cheese

"How much are they?" Donald asked as we stood in the heart of a stone barn in the hinterlands of Provence, surrounded by horned animals whose eyes were focused, unblinking, on us. Ethel, our three-year-old daughter, held my hand. The animals pushed against me, nuzzling my thighs and nibbling at the edge of my jacket. In the faint light cast by the single lightbulb suspended from the ceiling, I could see the dark mass of goats stretching toward the recesses of the barn and feel their slow but steady pressure as they pushed closer and closer. My nostrils filled with their pungent odor and the fragrance of the fresh hay on the barn floor, with the faintly damp, earthy aroma of the floor itself, and with the scent of all the animals that had preceded them in the ancient barn. The heat of their bodies intensified the smell, and although it was a cold November day, the barn was warm and cozy. Its earthy aromas were homey and comforting.

"Eh, ma foi. It's hard to decide. How many do you want? They're all pregnant. They were with the buck in September and October. They'll kid in February and March." The shepherd, a woman, leaned heavily on her cane, making her look older. She was dressed in layers of black, including black cotton stockings, the kind you see in movies set in prewar France, her only color a dark blue parka and a gold cross at her throat. A black wool scarf tied under her chin covered her hair.

We wanted to have enough goats to make a living. French friends had told us that we could make a living with the cheese produced from the milk of twenty to thirty goats.

"Why are you selling them?" I asked.

"Oh, I'm getting too old to keep so many. I have more than thirty." She looked around and then pointed at a large, sleek goat, russet and white. "I can sell you that one. Look at her. She's a beauty. Reinette, the little queen, I call her. She's a good milker, about four years old. Always has twins, too."

She moved across the barn and grabbed the goat by one horn, put her cane under her arm, and pulled back the goat's lips. "Take a look. See how good her teeth are. She's still young."

Reinette was released with a slap on her flank and went over to another goat standing aloof from the others. This one had a shaggy, blackish brown coat and scarred black horns that swept back high over her head.

"This is Lassie. She's *la chef* but getting old like me."

I expected the woman to cackle, but she didn't. Instead she sighed and said, "She's getting challenged by some of the younger goats now, but she'll be good for a few more years."

Donald walked over to the goat and stroked her head. She stared at him with her yellow eyes and inky-black pupils. "What others are you selling?"

"Mmmm. I could sell you Café au Lait." She pointed to a large, cream-colored goat with short hair and an arrogant look. "You might have trouble with her. You'll need to show her who's boss. She'd like to *be la chef,* take Lassie's place."

As if in response, Café au Lait crossed over to Lassie and gave her a hard butt in the side. Lassie whirled and butted her back, a solid blow to the head that echoed in the barn, bone on bone. Ethel pulled closer to me, holding my hand tightly, but kept her eyes on the battling goats.

"*Ça suffit! Arrete! Sales bêtes!*" the woman shouted at the goats, menacing them with her cane. Lassie faced down the larger Café au Lait, and the barn settled back into quiet.

She continued her sales pitch. "Café au Lait is only three years old, and last year she had triplets. She's a good goat." She showed us four more animals that she was willing to sell and kept up her spirited commentary on their characters and fertility patterns.

Donald and the woman agreed on a price of 350 francs each, and he made arrangements to pick up the beginning of our goat herd in two days. We all shook hands and said goodbye and then wound our way back toward the square where we had parked our car. I made sure Ethel's knitted cap, a yellow-and-orange-striped one of her choosing, was tied snugly beneath her chin, then pulled up the hood on my jacket and put my gloves back on.

As we walked through the narrow *ruelles,* the tiny streets of the near-abandoned village, Donald quietly remarked on the ghostly feeling of the crumbling houses with their fallen roofs exposing rotted wooden beams and piles of fallen stones. Wild berry canes pushed through some of the ruins and fig trees had taken possession of others.

It was hard to imagine Esparron-de-Verdon as a thriving village, and impossible not to think of the woman and her goats living there as relics of the past, clinging to a way of life that was long gone.

Surely what we were doing was something different. After all, we had bought a farmhouse in the country, not in an abandoned village, and we were college graduates. Donald even had a degree in animal husbandry, and while we were going to make traditional French cheese, we would bring modern methods to our technique, or so we thought. I was a little scared, though. We didn't have a lot of money, and we needed to succeed.

First, we had to learn how to make cheese. Our USDA pamphlets, directed at large-scale commercial milk production and cheese making for the United States market, didn't discuss small-scale production of cheese from raw goat's milk. So far no one, including the woman who had just sold us our first goats, had been able to tell me exactly what to do other than add rennet to milk.

"Mommy, can we have chickens and rabbits, too?" Ethel asked as we passed a ramshackle chicken coop made of corrugated tin and chicken wire and utilizing the three remaining walls of one of the sturdier ruins. Her favorite toys were her rubber farm animals, and she was delighted by the idea of having real animals, in addition to our dog, Tune (short for Petunia), which we had brought from California.

"Shh," I said, "not so loud." The silence was strong and heavy, and I sensed it was best to leave it unruptured.

I bent down toward her. "Yes, of course we can. We'll feed the chickens every day and collect their eggs. And build a nice house for them."

I wasn't so sure about rabbits. Keeping rabbits meant having to kill them for meat. I knew that on a real farm, the kind we were going to have, you couldn't just have animals as pets. I wasn't sure I was ready for that part yet. I had no farm experience, having grown up in a small Southern California beach town where surfing and sunbathing were the primary occupations. Chickens I could easily see—they had been part of my original vision when I imagined life in rural Provence, along with long, slow days of cooking, reading, writing, and sewing, with the occasional visit to Paris and trips to Italy and Spain, countries Donald and I had fallen in love with during our one-year honeymoon when we were students seven years before.

Reality Sets In

The first few weeks with our nascent goat herd were difficult, and we were on a steep learning curve. They wanted to roam and eat at their leisure, and we couldn't let them. The fields in the small valley below our house belonged to a farmer and were planted with winter wheat. He certainly wouldn't appreciate his crop being eaten to the quick by goats. On the far side of the valley, a vast pine and oak forest stretched to the north and west. If the goats ever reached the forest, we were sure we would never find them. That left only the hectare of land surrounding the house where the goats could feed, and that had to be under our supervision.

We didn't have an enclosure, so we had to devise some means to keep them under control. We tried taking the goats out on leashes that Donald had made using thick nylon cord and heavy-duty, twist-top hooks fastened to their collars. They not only ate the grass but also pulled us behind them as they climbed the pear and mulberry trees next to the house, chewing on the bark, and fought to get at the oaks and juniper on the neighbor's hillside. I still have the scar on my knee from the rock Café au Lait dragged me over one morning.

Next Donald filled old tires with cement to serve as anchors for the leashes. The Americans' goat anchors quickly became the talk of the area as word spread from the postman whose brother owned the only bar in the village. No anchors could hold those goats though. They would invariably head down to the field of appetizing green wheat, their weighted tires thudding behind them, with Donald and me following, trying to bring the goats back home.

We gave up on the tires and attached each goat to a metal stake we sunk deep into the ground. This was marginally more successful. Fortunately the cold weather and their advancing pregnancies made the goats increasingly content to snuggle in the warm barn and eat the alfalfa and barley we fed them.

French Shepherd's Pie with Celery Root and Potato Topping

Serves 4 to 6

Shepherd's pie, a traditional British dish, is made with meat—usually ground beef or lamb—and vegetables, covered with a thick layer of mashed potatoes and then lightly browned in the oven to make a crust. In this version, the topping is a combination of mashed potatoes and pungent celery root.

Celery root has a somewhat intimidating appearance. It is not at all obvious to the uninitiated how it is used in the kitchen. When I was a student in Aix-in-Provence, before Donald and I were married there, my French roommate taught me that once the whorled and callused skin of the celery root was removed, the flesh could be cooked or eaten raw in any number of different ways. An inexpensive winter root, its strong flavor and interesting texture made it frequent fare in our kitchen and also in the inexpensive restaurants we frequented.

4 tablespoons butter
1½ to 2 pounds ground lamb
½ onion, minced
2 carrots, peeled and cut into small pieces
3 fresh bay leaves or 1 dried bay leaf
1½ teaspoons sea salt
1½ teaspoons freshly ground black pepper
1 tablespoon all-purpose flour
1 cup beef stock
4 potatoes, peeled and quartered
2 medium-size or 1 large celery root, peeled and cut into 1-inch cubes
¼ cup whole milk
1 egg
1 teaspoon chopped fresh thyme

Melt 1 tablespoon of the butter in a large skillet over medium-high heat. Add the lamb and brown slightly on all sides, about 10 minutes. Remove to a bowl with a slotted spoon. Add the onion and carrots to the pan and sauté until the onion is soft and translucent, about 5 to 7 minutes. Return the meat to the pan. Add the bay leaves, sprinkle with 1 teaspoon each of the salt, pepper, and flour, and continue to cook, stirring constantly. The flour will start to brown on the bottom of the pan, but don't let it burn. Let it become very dark brown, as it is the browning of the flour that will eventually give the stew its rich, dark color. This will take 6 to 8 minutes. Stirring the meat and scraping the pan bottom, add the stock, a little at a time, until all the bits of browned flour are freed from the pan bottom and mixed into the liquid. Cover the pan, reduce the heat, and simmer until the flavors are blended and the sauce has thickened, about 15 minutes.

While the lamb is cooking, boil the potatoes and celery root in water to cover until tender, about 30 minutes.

Drain the potatoes and celery root, reserving ¼ cup of the cooking water, and place them in a bowl. Add the reserved cooking water, the milk, 2 tablespoons of the butter, egg, the remaining ½ teaspoon each salt and pepper, and the thyme. Whisk all the ingredients until well blended and fairly smooth.

Preheat an oven to 375 degrees F. To assemble the pie, put the stew in an ovenproof casserole and spoon the potato mixture evenly over the top to cover completely. Cut the remaining 1 tablespoon butter into bits and dot the topping with the bits. Place the casserole in the preheated oven until the topping is slightly browned and the stew is bubbling, 15 to 20 minutes.

Cherry Tomato Pasta with Fresh Goat Cheese

Serves 3 or 4

We had lots of fresh goat cheese when we kept the goats, and in summer this was an easy and inexpensive dish to make. I still make it now, but with purchased goat cheese. The fresh goat cheese added to the hot pasta and fresh tomatoes melts and binds with the tomatoes' juice and olive oil to form a creamy and delicate sauce.

1½ cups halved, very ripe, sweet cherry tomatoes, preferably a mixture of red and yellow
2 cloves garlic, minced
1 teaspoon sea salt
1 teaspoon freshly ground black pepper
¼ cup minced fresh basil
2 tablespoons extra virgin olive oil
10 ounces dried fettuccine or other pasta
2 ounces fresh goat cheese, crumbled

Place the cherry tomatoes in the bottom of a pasta serving bowl and stir in the garlic, salt, pepper, half of the basil, and the olive oil. Set aside.

Bring a large pot of salted water to a boil. Add the pasta and cook until just tender. Drain.

Immediately add the hot pasta to the bowl holding the tomatoes and stir in the goat cheese. Toss until the cheese has melted and a sauce has formed.

Garnish with the remaining basil and serve at once.

Warm Fig and Goat Cheese Bread Pudding

Serves 4

As the figs soak into the bread, their sweetness will be complemented by the light acidity of the goat cheese. If you use croissants or brioches, the dessert will be sweeter than if made with bread. Since leftover, stale bread is practically a food group in France, this is a quick dish and one that can be made with different types of fruit.

2½ tablespoons unsalted butter

8 stale baguette slices, or 2 croissants or brioches, torn into large pieces

1 egg, beaten

2 tablespoons sugar

⅔ cup milk

8 large, soft ripe figs, any kind

½ cup water

1 teaspoon fresh thyme leaves

1 ounce very fresh goat cheese

1 teaspoon fresh lemon juice

1 teaspoon finely grated lemon zest

Preheat an oven to 375 degrees F. Using 1 tablespoon of the butter, grease 4 individual ramekins, each about 6 inches in diameter and 2 inches deep. Divide the bread pieces equally among the prepared ramekins. In a bowl, whisk together the egg, sugar, and milk. Pour the mixture over the bread, dividing it equally. Set aside.

Chop 2 of the figs and put them in a small saucepan with the water and thyme. Bring to a boil and cook until the liquid is reduced by about one-third and the syrup has formed. Remove from the heat and set aside. Cut the remaining figs lengthwise into quarters and strew them equally over the 4 ramekins. Top with the fig syrup, dividing it evenly. With the back of a wooden spoon, press down on the figs. Dot the ramekins with the remaining 1½ tablespoons butter.

Bake until the custard has set and the figs are soft, about 20 minutes. Meanwhile, in a bowl, mix together the goat cheese, lemon juice, and half of the lemon zest. Five to 7 minutes before the fig dessert has finished baking, spread each ramekin with an equal amount of the goat cheese mixture. Serve hot or at room temperature, garnished with the remaining lemon zest.

We Experience *La France Profound*

We needed more goats, however, and someone told us that two shep-
herding brothers at La Motte, about forty minutes away, had some
goats to sell. The Audibert brothers, legends in the area, could be
seen during the winter months driving through the villages in their
ancient black Citroën, the kind in old French gangster movies, berets
pulled low on their heads, accompanied by their "housekeeper," a
flashily dressed, dark-haired woman who lived with them.

They still practiced *la grande transhumance*, driving their sheep and
goats on foot from the hot plateaus and valleys of southern Provence to
the alpine pastures in the north for the summer and then returning to
the valleys in late fall to overwinter the animals and let them lamb in
the milder south. In the winter, they installed themselves in La Motte,
in a huge stone farmhouse with a *bergerie* large enough to hold the
thousand head of sheep that made up their *troupeau*, or herd.

As we pulled up in front of the farmhouse, we saw the Citroën
parked under the single, unpruned mulberry tree, with a sheepdog tied
to it, and we knew we were in the right place. We went up the uneven
stone steps to the partially open front door. The response to our knock-
ing was a deep "*Entrez.*"

The room was lit only by the open door, a small window to the east,
and the glowing embers of a fire on the hearth. As we stepped in, I was
assailed by the odor of garlic and damp wool. One of the brothers sat at a

bare wooden table, a bottle of wine, some bread, and a dry sausage in front of him.

"Sit down," he said, waving his knife. "Some wine?" He got up and took three glasses off a wooden shelf above the sink. He was tall but not heavy, dark skinned and movie-star handsome, the kind of handsome where the dark shadow of a beard is omnipresent and the deep-set eyes are both vulnerable and arrogant. He was wearing a vintage black pin-striped vest and a wrinkled white shirt loosely tucked into black woolen pants, the style that men wore in the 1920s and 1930s, with buttons and flap. I could see a heavy, dark brown wool shepherd's cape hanging on the rear wall where it faded into the soot.

I was transfixed by the presence of a power that came from the man's place in the transhumance, making the same treks over the same *drailles*, or trails, that the Roman shepherds had made two thousand years before. To me, the Audibert brothers and others like them were part of the living history of Europe.

After a glass of the rough red wine and a few pieces of sausage plucked from the tip of the proffered knife, we answered some casual questions about being Americans and asked him about the goats.

"We're not going to do the transhumance anymore, so we don't need all our goats. Stay here all year. Settle down. Lots of people are doing that. Get tired of being up in those mountains. Good to be here. Got villages, music, cafés. Besides, people want lambs and sheep all year now. Used to be just spring." He sunk back in his chair, as if exhausted by such a long speech.

"Well, we're interested in buying some goats. We have seven, but need about a dozen or so more," Donald said.

"Come on, then. Let's go see them." He pushed up from the chair and grabbed the parka hanging behind it, leaving the shepherd's cape behind.

Donald, Ethel, and I followed him to the barn. It was built of stones, long, low, and sloping with a red tile roof, the kind you could still see then in the depths of inner Provence, where little had changed over the centuries and where people eked a subsistence living off the scrappy land. When we walked into the barn, the sheep, hundreds of them, fat with their winter coats, stayed bunched together, their bleating newborn lambs close to them, but the goats immediately came up to investigate us.

"Mommy, Daddy, look at all those lambs! Aren't they cute? Do you think we could get one? Do you? To keep the chickens we're going to get company."

"Shh. Not now. Maybe later. We have to get our goats first. Look at all these goats. Do you think they are as pretty as ours?" I had become quite attached to our goats once I had come to know their personalities.

Like our own goats, the Audibert goats were a mixture of colors and profiles. Some had horns; others not. Some had beards and wattle; others not. In our research on goats and cheese making, we had learned about the main breeds of good milkers: Saanen, Alpine, Nubian. But none of these goats we were seeing, or the ones we already had, looked like those, and when we asked about the specific breed, we just got a shrug. *"Ils sont des chevres du pays."* They're just goats from around here. I asked myself if these scruffy-looking animals would really produce enough milk for us to make cheese. It was clear that the first goats we purchased had lived a life of casual luxury compared to these goats.

Suddenly, M. Audibert walked away from the goats and went over to the huddled sheep and picked up something. "Here, this is for the little girl." He put a tiny black lamb into Ethel's arms.

"Feed it with a bottle. Warm milk. Its mother died."

"*Merci*." Ethel beamed, saying "Thank you" in French as we had taught her to do, and cradled the lamb close to her, its gawky legs dangling beneath her arms as she stroked its silky coat.

"Look, Mommy! Isn't it cute? He's soft, too. Feel." She held him toward me to stroke. It was true. His coat was soft and smooth, but he was so tiny. I could feel his ribs and his little heart thumping beneath them. Ethel cuddled and talked to her lamb while we looked at the goats M. Audibert was willing to sell. We took all twelve of them, agreeing to his asking price of 250 francs each, 100 francs less than the first goats. I hoped we were getting a good deal. He said he and his brother would deliver them to us within a day or two. We shook hands and walked to our car, thanking him again for the lamb.

Goat Cheese with *Herbes de Provence* and Olive Oil

This is the simplest appetizer I know, yet it is also among the best. This is a fine way to show off just-milled, new olive oil. Serve the cheese with crackers or thin slices of baguette. Take a log or a round of fresh goat cheese and put it on a serving platter. Sprinkle it generously with *herbes de Provence*, a little coarse sea salt, and some freshly ground black pepper. Finally, drizzle it with a good quality extra-virgin olive oil.

One 8-ounce round or log fresh goat cheese
1 teaspoon *herbes de Provence*
1 pinch course sea salt
1 pinch freshly ground pepper
1 drizzle extra-virgin olive oil

Fava Bean Toasts

Serves 4 to 6

Favas start out so small and tender that you can eat them right out of the pod. As time passes, they get larger and tougher. For this simple dish, you'll need to judge the blanching time according the tenderness of the beans. You want the beans tender but not mushy.

1 pound fava beans
1 drizzle extra-virgin olive oil
Sea salt to taste
Freshly ground pepper to taste
12 baguette slices
1 clove garlic, peeled
Fresh thyme or chive blossoms to garnish
Shell beans. You'll have about 1 to 1½ cups.

Bring a pot of salted water to a boil. Add the beans and cook anywhere from 30 seconds to 2 or 3 minutes, depending upon the beans. Drain and put in ice water to stop the cooking. Slip the skins off the beans.

Put the beans in a bowl and crush them with the back of a fork. Drizzle in some extra-virgin olive oil, just enough to make a spread. Taste and add sea salt and freshly ground black pepper to your taste. Grill or toast baguette slices. Rub the hot toasts with a garlic clove and drizzle with a little olive oil. Spread the toasts with the fava beans, and if you want, garnish with fresh thyme or chive blossoms, which appear in the garden at the same time that fava beans are ready to harvest.

Quince Poached in Vanilla Syrup

Serves 4

Quince, which is astringent when raw, absorbs other flavors when it's poached. It also turns a lovely golden amber color. Serve it as a dessert, a condiment, or a breakfast fruit, warm or chilled.

3 quinces
3 cups water
3 cups sugar
1 vanilla bean about 8 inches long

Peel and core the quinces and cut them into slices ½-inch thick. Combine the water and the sugar in a sauce pan and bring to a boil over medium high heat. Slit the vanilla bean lengthwise and add it to the syrup along with the quinces slices. Reduce the heat to low and simmer until the quinces are tender and can easily be pierced with the tines of the fork, about 20 minutes. Remove and let cool. Store covered in the refrigerator for up to a week. Makes about 4 cups.

The Milk Is Coming Soon,
But How to Make the Cheese?

As the bellies of our goats swelled with their babies, we set about the now-urgent task of trying to figure out how to make cheese. When the Audibert brothers delivered the goats, I asked them how they made their cheese. They looked at me as if I were simple minded.

"On trait les chèvres, met un peu de préssure dans le lait. Le prochain jour c'est caillé, et on met le caillé dans les moules. On les tourne le lendemain. Le troisième jour on les tourne encore et met du sel. Le quatrième jour ils sont faits."

In other words, milk the goats, add some rennet, let it curdle overnight, ladle the curds into molds. The next day, turn the cheeses, and the day after, turn them again and salt them. On the fourth day, they're ready. This seemed a little vague to me, especially compared with the technical material I had been reading from the United States, which presented cheese making as a very precise endeavor.

One day, as I was leaving the tiny *épicerie*, or grocery store, where I had gone to buy some rice, a woman spoke to me.

"I hear you have goats," she said.

She introduced herself as Mme. Lacroste. She was just a little older than I was, with shoulder-length, dark, curly hair, a bright smile, and the work-roughened hands of a *paysanne*. I knew she was the wife of the man who owned one of the larger farms. They lived in a hamlet next to their vineyards.

"I remember when my parents had goats, and my mother made us fresh cheese. After the war she got rid of them. No one has goats anymore. I hear you are going to make cheese."

"Yes, but I'm having trouble finding out exactly how to make the cheese," I laughed.

"Do you want to meet my mother and ask her? I don't remember myself. I never made it; she did."

I accepted this very kind offer, and we arranged that I would come by her house that afternoon about four o'clock and go together to her mother's house.

Mme. Lacroste was sitting on her porch, knitting, when I arrived. She got up immediately to greet me, putting her knitting on the chair. "*Bonjour, Madame*," she said and shook my hand.

"Shall we go?"

"Yes, yes, I'm ready." She was friendly but seemed more abrupt than other people I had dealt with thus far, brusquely buttoning up her rust red sweater over a blue printed dress and picking up a willow basket lined with newspaper next to her chair.

"This way. My mother lives just down that road," she said, pointing, "at the edge of the hamlet. In the house I grew up in and my grandmother, too. I was an only child. Good thing I married a farmer. Those are our vineyards." She swept her arm in a gesture that encompassed all the vineyards in view, now shorn of their grapes and their leaves mottled with red and yellow. It was a large vineyard for the area, maybe four or five hectares.

The sky was a brilliant blue, as it often is in Provence during November and December, and a recent rain had washed everything, rendering the colors sharp and clear. It was strange to be walking down a dirt road with the wife of a Provençal farmer to learn about goat cheese. Not so long ago, I was walking with other graduate students at UC San Diego, heading for lectures or classes across a new campus with modernist buildings of concrete and glass. Eucalyptus, bougainvillea, and long green lawns were the backdrop of conversation, not vineyards, olive trees, and forest.

Standing next to a sprawling two-story stone house was a woman in a bright blue scarf, holding her weathered face to the sun. Her black dress was indistinguishable from those worn by all the older women,

remnants of a period when widow's weeds were required, I suppose, but her sweater was deep pink, and her heavy gold necklace reflected the sunlight against her thinning skin.

"*Mémé!*" Mme. Lacroste called out, "I've brought a visitor to *Maman*. An American. Remember the Americans? They came during the war."

Both hands were resting on the top of a cane. As we drew closer, I could see the gold bracelet on her wrist and a thick, worn gold wedding ring. Her eyes, covered with a bluish film, were set deep in her wrinkled face. Her thin cheeks rounded as she smiled.

"Ah, ma petite! Comment vas-tu?" She leaned her face slightly toward what she must have sensed was our direction, and my companion kissed her grandmother on both cheeks, and then introduced me.

"C'est Madame l'Americaine. She's keeping goats and is going to make goat's-milk cheese."

The old woman let go of her cane with one hand and stretched it out in my direction. I took it. Her handshake was firm, her hand warm and smooth.

"Yes, yes, I remember the Americans. One in particular." She laughed. "Very big and handsome, those American boys. Much better than the filthy Germans. The Germans took our house, you know. That's right. They were here almost six months, four of them. Ate our chickens, our food, everything. You can still see the bullet holes on the barn where they tried to shoot our pigeons."

The German soldiers had been right here, at this farm. What stories could be told, I thought. I wanted to ask her when they came and how they looked and what happened to them, and many more questions, but my language skills were not quite up to it. I also wasn't sure that questioning her on the subject at our first meeting, or ever, would be the correct thing to do, so I simply made some sympathetic sounds.

Provence is like that. Whenever I am there, I bump into history, all of it connected. I suppose I'm now part of that history, too: the American who kept goats.

Onion Pancakes with Dandelion Greens and Bacon

Serves 4

When we lived in Provence with our goats, we often gathered the abundant wild dandelions, as our neighbors had taught us to do. We mostly used them for salads, but they can be cooked as well, or wilted as they are here.

Batter:
1 cup all-purpose flour
2½ teaspoons baking powder
½ teaspoon sea salt
2 eggs
1¼ cups milk
3 tablespoons butter, melted and cooled
½ cup finely chopped green onions
Vegetable oil

Topping:
1 bunch dandelion greens or spinach, stems removed
16 slices bacon
6 tablespoons butter
¼ cup finely chopped fresh parsley
1 tablespoon fresh lemon juice

To make the batter, sift the flour into a bowl. Return it to the sifter, add the baking powder and salt, and resift the flour into the bowl.

Beat the eggs and milk together in a large bowl until well mixed. Stir in the butter and then add the flour mixture. Beat the batter until it is smooth and free of lumps. Stir in the green onions. Preheat an oven to 200 degrees F.

Heat a frying pan or griddle until it is medium-hot and grease it lightly with vegetable oil. For each pancake, ladle about ¼ cup of the batter into the heated pan or onto the griddle. Cook the pancakes until bubbles form on the tops, and the bottoms are golden brown, 2 to 3 minutes. Turn and cook until the second side is golden, 2 to 3 minutes. Remove the pancakes to a heated dish and place in the oven. Repeat with the remaining batter. You should have 12 thin pancakes in all.

Arrange the greens on a steamer rack placed over gently boiling water. Cover and steam the greens until they are tender, 3 or 4 minutes. Remove the greens from the steamer and julienne lengthwise. Keep warm in the oven.

Meanwhile, cook the bacon in a frying pan over medium-high heat until crisp. Drain on paper towels and keep warm in the oven.

In a small pan, melt the butter. Stir in the parsley and lemon juice and keep warm over very low heat.

For each serving, place a pancake on a dinner plate. Place a layer of the greens and 2 strips of the bacon on the pancake. Top with a second pancake and repeat the layering of the greens and bacon. Finally, place a third pancake on top. When all 4 of the pancake stacks are made, pour some of the warm parsley butter over each stack. Serve immediately.

Gratin of Belgian Endive

Serves 4 to 6

A curious vegetable, Belgian endive is really the end result of two stages of growth, one in the field and the other under forced conditions. In the first stage, the seeds are planted in early summer. They produce a huge, leafy, very bitter plant that looks somewhat like a monstrous, hairy spinach. In the late fall, stage two begins. The green leafy tops are cut away to within an inch of the crown. The roots of the plant are dug up, buried in a mixture of sand and soil, and kept in a cool, preferably dark place. In about three weeks, stored energy in the roots produces a second growth of leaves that overlap one another, forming torpedo-shaped heads. These are ivory white and very, very tender, with the slight bitterness that I like so much.

Belgian endive leaves are delicious raw in salads, and they mix especially well with winter fruits and nuts. I like them best cooked in this gratin dish. But, if I am rushed, I will just toss a few heads, properly called *chicons*, into a pan alongside a roasting chicken and simmer them in the juices.

8 small- to medium-size heads of Belgian endive
3½ tablespoons butter
3 tablespoons all-purpose flour
½ teaspoon sea salt
¼ teaspoon freshly grated nutmeg
⅛ teaspoon cayenne pepper
1 cup milk
¼ cup plus 1 tablespoon freshly grated Swiss cheese
4 ounces thinly sliced prosciutto
½ tablespoon freshly ground black pepper

Preheat the oven to 375 degrees F. With a small, sharp knife, cut out the inverted V-shaped cores of the Belgian endives. (The core tends to be bitter.) Set aside.

To make the sauce, melt 2 tablespoons of butter in a heavy-bottomed saucepan over medium heat. When the butter begins to foam, remove the pan from the heat and whisk in the flour, salt, nutmeg, and cayenne pepper until a paste forms. Return the pan to medium heat and gradually whisk in the milk in a slow, steady stream. Reduce the heat to low and stir until there are no lumps. Simmer the sauce, stirring occasionally, until it becomes thick enough to coat the back of a spoon, about 10 minutes. Stir in the cheese and continue to cook only until the cheese has melted into the sauce, 2 to 3 minutes. Taste for seasoning and adjust with salt, if necessary.

Using ½ tablespoon of the butter, grease the bottom and sides of a shallow ovenproof casserole about 12 to 14 inches long and 8 inches wide, or just large enough to hold the Belgian endives, ham, and sauce. Arrange the Belgian endives in the casserole and top with the ham. Carefully pour the sauce over the top. Cut the remaining 1 tablespoon butter into small bits and dot the surface. Strew the 1 tablespoon grated cheese over the top. Bake in the preheated oven until done, 25 to 30 minutes. Sprinkle with pepper and serve hot.

Madame Rillier Invites Me
Into Her Kitchen

"*Maman*," Mme. Lacroste called as she headed toward the huge *potager*, the vegetable garden behind the house. There, her mother stood bent over a shovel, digging up what looked like onions. Rows of cabbages, greens, and beets stretched out around her in perfect symmetry. Every bit of the huge garden was filled with something growing. Like her mother, Madame Rillier was wearing a black dress, but her sweater was a somber, serviceable dark blue.

"I've come with the American, for you to tell her about cheese." Mme. Lacroste turned to me and said, "My grandmother made cheese, too, of course, but now, no matter what question you ask her, she only talks about certain things, like the Germans, her dead husband, her wedding trip to Nice."

"*Bonjour, Madame Rillier*," I said to my companion's mother. She gave me a no-nonsense handshake, and I understood where Mme. Lacroste had acquired her manner.

"So. You want to make cheese our way. No cheese in America?" She put her hands on her hips and looked me up and down.

"Yes, there's cheese, but not goat cheese. Not like the French home-made goat cheese." The term *artisanal* was not yet in my vocabulary.

That would come twenty years later, with the beginning of the boom of artisanal foods in the United States.

"Well, I'm glad someone is going to make it again. No one does anymore." No wonder I couldn't find any cheese, I thought. No one is making it.

"I used to have seven or eight goats, milked them, and then made cheese," Mme. Rillier said. "I sold the extra cheeses. A few others around did the same. The others are dead now, and it got to be too much for me to do by myself. But I'll tell you how to do it. Come inside."

Mme. Rillier pushed aside the bowls of soggy bread and food scraps set outside for chickens, a dog, and cats, all of which were hovering nearby, and we followed her through a swinging screen door into the kitchen. The dog, a brown and white spaniel, was on a chain, and the circumference of the ground within his reach was worn bare with his pacing. "We've got to keep him on a chain; otherwise he runs off. Loose dogs get shot. My husband goes hunting with him."

This was my first invitation into a family home kitchen since our arrival in Provence, and it wasn't at all what I expected.

No authentic-looking cooper pans gleaming over a well-used fire-place, no exposed-wood ceiling beams, no soapstone or red-tile sink, no terra-cotta pots filled with olives, no bright Provençal printed fabric. In short, this was not like the kitchen in the farmhouse we had rented one summer outside Aix-en-Provence.

Over the next few years, as I came to know various farmhouse and modest village kitchens, I would find most of them very much like this one. Many had been modernized during the 1950s or 1960s, with some indoor plumbing and electricity installed, and a small, tubular white

enamel water heater hanging over a utilitarian white sink set in faux granite or tiled cement. The walls of these kitchens were painted with multiple layers of pale green or cream-colored enamel, and the floors were red tiles if old, or tiles of inexpensive granite composite if new. An oil- or wood-burning stove both for cooking and for heat was set where a fireplace had once reigned, with the stove's pipe cut into the chimney flue. Sometimes the mantel was still there, with the pipe stretching beneath it. Somewhere, there would be a propane-fueled, two-burner stovetop or perhaps a modest new stove as well as the oil- or wood-burning one. Often, an overstuffed chair was in a corner and a small *canapé*, or couch, stood against a wall.

It was early winter, and Mme. Rillier's kitchen was warm. Something that smelled of onions and garlic was cooking in a hissing pressure cooker on the back of the stove. A stew maybe, or dried beans, I thought. Greens freshly cut from the garden lay on the sink, along with the bucket of onions she had just brought in.

Couscous Salad with
Chili-Mint *Harissa*

Serves 4 to 6

Properly speaking, couscous is semolina flour that is mixed with salted water, then formed into tiny round pellets, and finally cooked by steaming. Couscous is also a generic term for any of the numerous vegetable-and-meat stews of North African origin that are served with the grain, which is generally steamed over the simmering broth of the stew. The traditional accompaniment to these stews is *harissa*, a spicy sauce made from crushed dried chili peppers, olive oil, salt, and sometimes garlic and cumin, which is then thinned with broth from the simmering stew.

Couscous also makes a wonderful base for salads. Here the cooked, cooled grains are tossed with liberal amounts of chopped tomato, cucumber, and green onions, minced fresh mint and parsley and a bit of olive oil, lemon juice, salt, and pepper. The spicy *harissa* makes good use of the abundant mint in the garden and the last of the dried chilies from the previous summer.

1½ cups chicken stock
1½ cups couscous
2 tablespoons butter, cut into small pieces
5½ tablespoons extra-virgin olive oil
4 tomatoes, peeled, seeded, and chopped
3 cucumbers, peeled, seeded, and chopped
3 green onions, chopped
¼ cup minced fresh mint
¼ cup minced fresh parsley
¼ cup fresh lemon juice
¼ teaspoon sea salt
½ teaspoon freshly ground black pepper
Fresh mint sprigs for garnish

Harissa:
¼ cup fresh mint leaves
2 cloves garlic, crushed
1 cup chicken stock
1 small, dried red chili pepper or 2 fresh serrano chili peppers
Sea salt to taste

Bring the chicken stock to a boil in a medium-size saucepan. Stir in the couscous, cover and cook over very low heat for 5 minutes. Remove the pan from the heat and let the couscous stand, covered, until all the liquid has been absorbed, about 5 minutes. Add the butter to the couscous and fluff carefully with a fork to separate the grains. I use my fingertips as well. Add 1½ tablespoons of the olive oil and fluff again. The idea is for each pellet to be separate and fluffy. Let cool at room temperature.

Add the tomatoes, cucumbers, green onions, mint, and parsley to the couscous and fluff the ingredients together. In a small bowl, mix together the remaining 4 tablespoons olive oil, the lemon juice, salt and pepper. Pour it over the couscous mixture. Fluff one more time. Set the salad aside.

To make the *harissa*, in a small saucepan bring the mint, garlic, and chicken stock to a boil. Reduce the heat and simmer for 10 minutes. Remove and discard the stems and seeds from the dried or fresh chilies and add the chilies to the stock. Increase the heat to high and reduce the stock mixture by half, which will take 5 to 10 minutes. Transfer the mixture to a blender or food processor and purée until smooth.

Serve the salad chilled or at room temperature. Garnish with mint sprigs. Serve the *harissa* on the side in a separate bowl.

NOTE: Do not use instant (cooked) couscous, as it is difficult to fluff up.

Leek and Salt Cod Gratin

Serves 4

I first had this on New Year's Eve in Provence, when our neighbors the Fines invited us to celebrate with them. Eating it was a completely new experience for me, as I had never eaten either leeks or salt cod before, and certainly not in combination with a creamy sauce and gratinéed. It is one of the most memorable dishes I have ever had.

1 pound boneless salt cod
1 tablespoon extra-virgin olive oil
4 tablespoons butter
1 cup minced leeks, including some of the tender greens
2 tablespoons all-purpose flour
¼ teaspoon sea salt
½ teaspoon freshly ground black pepper
¼ teaspoon cayenne pepper
¾ cup milk
¼ cup freshly grated Gruyère cheese
2 tablespoons chopped fresh parsley
1 cup salt-cured black olives

Rinse the salt cod, which has already been salt-cured, under running water for 10 minutes. Soak the salt cod in cold water and cover overnight. The next morning, change the water and let the cod stand covered for 4 hours. Change the water again and let stand for another 2 hours. Rinse the cod under cold running water for 10 minutes. The cod will begin to plump up as it refreshes. Taste for saltiness. The actual length of time you will need to soak the cod will depend upon how much salt was used when it was cured. When desalted, the taste will be mild and somewhat sweet but should still retain the characteristic salty taste.

Put the soaked cod in a shallow casserole or frying pan and add water to cover. Bring to a boil and reduce the heat to low. Cook just until the fish flakes when poked with a fork, 3 to 4 minutes. Remove from the water and let cool. When cool, separate into small flakes. If too salty, it may be rinsed again under cold running water. Be sure to squeeze all water from the flakes. They should be quite dry before adding them to the gratin. Set aside.

Heat the olive oil and 1 tablespoon of the butter in a skillet over medium heat. Add the leeks and sauté until they become translucent, about 5 minutes. Remove from the heat and set aside.

To make the sauce, melt 2 tablespoons of the butter in a heavy-bottomed saucepan over medium heat. When the butter begins to foam, remove the pan from the heat and whisk in the flour, salt, black pepper, and cayenne pepper until a paste forms. Return the pan to medium heat and gradually whisk in the milk in a steady stream. Reduce the heat to low and stir until there are no lumps. Simmer the sauce, stirring occasionally, until it becomes thick enough to coat the back of a spoon, about 10 minutes. Stir in the cheese and continue to cook only until the cheese melts into the sauce, 2 to 3 minutes. Taste for seasonings and adjust for salt, if necessary.

Preheat the oven to 375 degrees F. Combine the flaked cod, leeks and their cooking juices, the sauce, and the parsley. Butter an ovenproof dish, just large enough to hold the mixture. Pour the cod mixture into the baking dish and dot with the olives. Cut the remaining tablespoon of butter into tiny bits and scatter over the top. Bake in the preheated oven until a crisp, golden crust forms, 20 to 30 minutes.

New Harvest Chickpeas with Garlic Sausage

Serves 6 to 8

The chickpeas grown in Haute Provence are the size of the tip of a little finger, quite a bit smaller than the ones we see bagged in supermarkets. In late fall, as soon as they are harvested and cleaned, they begin to appear at the open markets and at small, local épiceries packaged in brown paper bags with *pois chiche* handwritten on the front. They taste nutty and sweet and their texture remains a little bit crunchy, even when fully cooked and well seasoned with bay leaf, thyme, and winter savory. I can eat them by the bowlful, with nothing more than a green salad, fresh bread, and red wine. For a less rustic presentation, include grilled sausages, cut into pieces just before serving. As the chickpeas age, they dry slightly, so those used later in the year or from a previous year's harvest may take considerably longer to cook.

2 cups dried chickpeas
8 cups water
2 fresh bay leaves, or 1 dried
3 fresh thyme sprigs plus 1 tablespoon minced fresh thyme
1 teaspoon sea salt
1 teaspoon freshly ground black pepper
6 mild or spicy garlic sausages
1 tablespoon butter

Pick over the chickpeas, discarding any tiny stones or other impurities. If the chickpeas are not recently harvested, soak them overnight in water to cover. When ready to cook, drain them, rinse well and then place them in a saucepan with the water. Add the bay, thyme sprigs, salt, and pepper and bring to a boil. Reduce the heat to medium-low, half cover the pan, and cook until the chickpeas are soft to the bite, 2 to 3 hours. Remove from the heat and drain, reserving the liquid.

Return the liquid to the pan and bring to a boil over high heat. Boil until reduced by half. Meanwhile, prick the sausages with a fork, place them in a saucepan, and add water to cover. Bring to a boil over medium-high heat, reduce to medium-low, and simmer for 4 to 5 minutes. Drain. Melt the butter in a large skillet over medium heat. When it is foamy, add the sausages and sauté, turning as needed, until golden brown on all sides. Remove from the heat and cut into 1-inch pieces.

Return the chickpeas to the reduced liquid and add the sausages and their juices. Cook over medium heat until the chickpeas are hot. Ladle into warmed bowls and garnish with the minced thyme.

Fresh Berry Galette

Serves 4 to 6

These free-form galettes, essentially pastry dough wrappped around a fruit–pie like filling, are a typical home-style French dessert. You could use other fruits, such as sliced peaches, plums, or apricots.

1 ready-to-roll pie-crust dough
4 cups fresh blackberries
2 cups fresh raspberries
1 cup sugar
2 tablespoons cornstarch
2 teaspoons lemon juice
Zest from one medium lemon
1 egg lightly beaten
Extra sugar for sprinkling

Preheat oven to 400 degrees F and place a baking sheet on the lower rack. Roll out the pie-crust dough until it is 2 to 3 inches beyond the circumference of a pie pan and then gently lay it over the pie pan and press it down, allowing the extra dough to hang over the edge. Set aside.

In a large bowl, combine blackberries, raspberries, sugar, cornstarch, lemon juice, and lemon zest. Gently stir until evenly mixed and then pour the mixture into the pan lined with pie-crust dough.

Fold the extra dough up and over the filling, forming loose pleats. Brush the pleated dough with a light layer of egg and then sprinkle with sugar. Bake until the filling is bubbling and the crust is golden, about 25 minutes.

I Began to Learn About Making Goat Cheese

A collection of succulents sat in small pots on the windowsill. On the wall, above an overstuffed brown chair covered with a crocheted afghan in shades of orange, blue, and brown, hung a shotgun.

"Here," Mme. Rillier said, reaching into a cupboard. "This is a cheese mold." She held a cuplike ceramic object, glazed ocher on the inside, the terra-cotta of the outside unglazed. It was perforated with a regular pattern of small round holes. She reached deeper into the cupboard and brought out several more molds in various sizes.

"These are what I used. I think they might come in plastic now. Used to be someone in the village who made all the clay things we needed—*daubières*, *tians*, casseroles, bowls, and these cheese molds. He died during the war."

The war again. It was still close to these people's lives, I realized. She would have been about twenty-five when the war ended, and her daughter was born during the war. I wondered again about the Germans. What was it like to live in this isolated place? German soldiers billeted in your house, your men gone to war or with *la Resistance*?

"You make your cheese right after milking, while the milk is warm. Don't let it cool off. Pour the milk into a big bowl or bucket and add the rennet."

This was the key moment for me. I quickly abandoned my imaginings about the war.

"How much rennet?"

"Just a tiny drop for, say, five liters. Not much. If you add too much, the cheese will be like rubber, full of holes and bitter."

"And then what?" I asked, afraid that she had finished.

"Then you cover the milk up and by morning it will be curdled. Or, if morning milk, curdled by dinner. Scoop the curd into the molds and set them out to drain. That's what the holes are for. The next day, salt the cheeses, turn them over, and let them drain another day. That's it."

"That's it? What about aging? Isn't the cheese awfully soft?"

"Of course it's soft. It's a fresh cheese. Every day you keep it, it gets older. Cheese is a living thing, you know, like wine. It changes, just like us, as it gets older. If you want an aged cheese, you keep it longer."

This didn't exactly correspond to the USDA guidance about aging cheeses.

"But if your cheeses are good, you won't have any to age. People will buy them right away. It's hard to get fresh cheese anymore. And we all remember it, right, Marie Pierre?" She turned to her daughter, who agreed.

"Well, that's it." Mme. Rillier put the cheese molds back into her cupboard.

I thanked her very much, and told Mme. Lacroste I could go back if she wanted to stay, which she did. I left mother and daughter in the kitchen.

The dog woke up to bark at me as I left, stretching and pulling on his chain. I stayed clear of his reach and made my way to the front of the house and back to the road slowly, trying to see as much of the *potager* as I could without appearing nosy. I kept my hands tucked deep in my pockets as I walked.

FÊTE DE LAVANDE

Any visitor who goes to Provence hopes to see the lavender fields in bloom, acres and acres of purple rows reaching to the horizon. In the flowering season, you can see cars pulled up alongside the lavender fields and people posing against the dramatic backdrop of intense purple. Trucks stacked high with freshly cut lavender ply the back roads, trailing a perfumed scent behind them. In the open markets, fresh lavender bouquets are sold for a brief time, and lavender honey is stacked high on the tables of the honey sellers. Across the country-side hand-painted roadside signs entice the visitor indicating "*produits de lavande ici*" with an arrow pointing the way.

In villages throughout Provençal lavender producing regions, there are *fêtes de lavande*, celebrating the local harvest. Depending on the location, lavender blooms in July and early August, and the fêtes correspond to local harvest time. The fêtes themselves vary from a collection of vendors' stalls selling lavender products to more elaborate affairs such as the one produced in Sault.

Every August 15, since 1985, the small rural village of Sault in the lavender region of the Vaucluse has celebrated the season with

a Fête de Lavande. Participating villagers and performers dress in traditional Provençal costumes of the eighteenth and nineteenth centuries and bring the past to life not only with parades, music, and dance, but with wagons full of lavender drawn by horses and mules, the mode which was used to transport the lavender in the days before tractors and trucks. There is even a lavender harvest contest. The contestants are outfitted with over-the-shoulder bags and hand sickles. They attack the blooming plants, cutting the tufts down to the leafy base, and load the bags with lavender, wielding the sickles as fast as they can while the crowd cheers them on

Vendors sell everything lavender related, and at 12:30 a multi-course "Country Lunch" of locally produced food is served on long community-style tables in the shade of the oak trees in the nearby woods of the Hippodrome du Deffends. Tickets, or subscriptions as they are called, must be purchased ahead and typically cost about twenty-one euros.

The vistas of rolling hills and plateaus of purple lavender are iconic symbols of Provence, but it wasn't always so. Lavender only became a cultivated crop after World War I, and even then the gathering of wild lavender, which was abundant, remained commercially viable until the late 1940s.

Prior to the commercial plantings of lavender, wild lavender, which has long been used in the production of perfume, was harvested on a first-come, first-served basis by local people, primarily women, and then purchased from them directly by perfume manufactures or by brokers. One of my neighbors in Provence told me of the times when, as a young girl recently emigrated from Calabria, Italy, she worked the lavender harvest on the Valensole Plateau, near Riez in the Alpes d'Haute Provence. Harvesting was done with a sickle, and the cut lavender was tied up in big linen bundles. The workers sometimes slept out under the stars and cooked food over a campfire, she told me. It sounds romantic, but it was actually arduous, back-breaking work. Today, the harvest is done mechanically.

As the perfume industry grew, so did the importance of lavender, and by the early part of the twentieth century, the gathering of wild lavender had an opening date and a closing date to control the harvest season. Small, portable distilleries were set up throughout the lavender-producing regions, primarily the Alpes d'Haute Provence, Vaucluse, and the Drome, and lavender distilling became a family enterprise.

The gathering of the wild lavender from the hillsides disappeared along with many of the small family distilleries. By far the greatest portion of the crop today goes to making perfume, pharmaceuticals, and soaps. The remainder ends up in the floral market for drying or for culinary use. *La lavande fine*, which is cultivated at higher altitudes, is making a comeback, however, because of the high quality of its fragrance and oil.

Rice, Tomato, and Olive Salad

Serves 4

In Provence, this salad made from the previous night's rice is served at midday. The olives lend their deep flavor to the otherwise bland rice, and the tomatoes—even wintertime ones—add texture and acidity. Other ingredients can be added, such as chopped sweet peppers, and basil can be used instead of parsley.

1½ to 2 cups cooked long-grain white rice, at room temperature
1 tomato, chopped
1 tablespoon balsamic vinegar
1 tablespoon extra-virgin olive oil
½ teaspoon freshly ground black pepper
½ teaspoon sea salt
¼ cup minced red or green onion
20 tart green or oil-cured black olives, pitted and chopped
¼ cup minced fresh parsley

Combine all the ingredients in a bowl. Turn gently with a wooden spoon until well mixed.

Honey and Lavender Glazed Chicken

Serves 4

The powerful flavors and fragrance of the herbs creates a tremendously woodsy tang mingled with sweetness. The skin of the chicken turns a glistening dark mahogany, while the meat beneath remains tender and fragrant. This is my version of a dish I had at Les Santons restaurant in Moustiers-Sainte-Marie.

4 teaspoons lavender flowers, crushed
2 teaspoons minced dried lavender stems
1 tablespoon fresh thyme leaves
2 teaspoons fresh or dried winter savory leaves
12 black peppercorns
1 teaspoon sea salt
4 chicken breast halves, bone-in, skin on
¼ cup strong-flavored honey, preferably lavender or acacia

Preheat the oven to 450 degrees F. In a mortar, grind together 2 teaspoons of the lavender flowers, the stems, thyme, winter savory, peppercorns, and salt. Rub each chicken breast half with about 1 teaspoon of the mixture. Place the chicken breasts, skin side up, on a baking sheet. Roast for 10 minutes. Remove from the oven and baste the chicken thoroughly with honey. Sprinkle all but 2 teaspoons of the remaining herb mixture evenly over the chicken breasts. Return to the oven, reduce the heat to 350 degrees F, and roast, basting frequently with the pan juices, until the juices run clear when a chicken breast is pierced with the tip of a knife, about 20 minutes longer. Frequent basting is important as the honey, once warm, pours off the chicken into the pan and regular basting ensures the honey flavor of the finished dish.

Remove from the oven and serve immediately, sprinkled with the remaining 2 teaspoons crushed lavender flowers.

Pumpkin Gratin

Serves 4 as a side dish

Musquée de Provence is the pumpkin found throughout Provence. Small ones weigh fifteen pounds, and large ones up to forty, but they are distinguished more by their appearance and flavor than by their size. The skin is the color of new copper with a finish of dull green, and the shape is squat and round, deeply and asymmetrically convoluted and lobed. After harvesting in late fall, the pumpkins are taken to the cave, or cellar, where they will keep until spring. When they are needed in the kitchen, a slice is cut, often only a lobe or two, and the rest is left in storage. In markets throughout the region, they are sold in the same manner by the slice. The pumpkins are displayed stacked, usually with one already sliced open and a sign indicating the price by the kilogram. The dense meat is bright orange, and after cooking, it has a nutty flavor and creamy texture.

2 pounds *Musquée de Provence* pumpkin, Sugar Pie pumpkin, or butternut squash
1½ tablespoons all-purpose flour
2 tablespoons fresh thyme leaves
½ teaspoon sea salt
1 teaspoon cayenne pepper or other ground dried chili pepper
3 tablespoons unsalted butter
2½ tablespoons extra-virgin olive oil
¼ cup grated Gruyère or Swiss cheese

Preheat the oven to 350 degrees F. Peel the squash, remove the seeds, and cut the flesh into ½-inch cubes. Place the cubes in a bowl and sprinkle them with the flour, thyme leaves, salt, and ground chili pepper. Coat the cubes by turning and tossing with two spoons. Place half of the butter in a small gratin dish, just large enough to hold the cubes snugly in a jumbled single layer. Pour the olive oil into the bottom of the baking dish. Transfer the coated squash to the dish. Cut the remaining butter into small pieces and dot the top of the gratin.

Bake until the squash is somewhat tender, about 45 minutes. Remove from the oven and sprinkle the cheese on top. Return to the oven and continue to cook until the squash is thoroughly tender when pierced with the tines of a fork, 10 to 15 minutes. Serve hot.

Failure upon Failure;
Then at Last, Success

Our second house in Provence, a rental, was in such a state of disrepair that it could have been called a ruin, but the roof was good and the payment low. It faced the southwest, and its ocher stones were bathed in light nearly all day, which I loved. The house had a well right beside it, and a fireplace inside, but no electricity. We installed new windows, a sink, a cooking counter to hold a two-burner propane cooktop, and a glass-paned door to let extra light into the single downstairs room that served as living room and kitchen.

Donald made us a bed with pieces of oak from an old, dismantled wine press, and we set it up in the big bedroom upstairs. A smaller room next to it became Ethel's room. A door from the big bedroom led directly into the loft behind it, giving us easy, dry access to the hay we fed the goats. Downstairs we put in a similar door from the kitchen into the barn so we would have the same easy, dry access to the goats themselves. I set up my small, screened cheese room in the space under the staircase, which was just large enough to hold the new draining and curing racks, plus a bucket to catch the whey.

Next to the spacious barn, we built an enclosure for the goats, using sturdy branches of oak and pine from the forest behind us, so the goats could come and go freely from the barn, yet be contained. Donald fashioned a manger inside for their hay, and by the time the first kids arrived we were as ready as we could be.

When we were settled, we invited some new friends for dinner: Denys Fine, the local schoolteacher, and his wife Georgette, both of whom were artists, had helped us with some of the work on the house; Mark and Nina Haag, an American couple we had met, were living in the village for the winter, had also helped us get settled, and had even taken care of the goats for us for several days when we had to go to Lyon to buy cheese-making supplies.

I grilled pork chops seasoned with wild rosemary in the fireplace. I had never cooked in a fireplace before, and although I relished the idea, I wasn't very skillful. Half of the chops were burned, partly because it was hard to see what I was doing by candlelight. The stuffed zucchini I cooked in my grandmother's cast-iron Dutch oven were overcooked, limp, and shriveled (besides being out of season). Fortunately I had bought a nut tart from the boulangerie for dessert, and there was wine and good conversation. For months afterward, we didn't have any more dinner guests, not because we didn't want to, but because we were too busy.

We had just enough time during the day to take care of our basic needs—food, warmth, clothing, and cleanliness, which meant hauling and boiling water and building a daily fire, among other things—and to tend the goats, milk them, and make cheese. However, not until Reinette had been in labor for more than ten hours did I begin to realize how closely our lives were tied to the animals we kept in the barn just behind our kitchen.

We left the kids with their mothers for two weeks, to give them a good start, and then we separated them, feeding the kids a mixture of powdered milk that we purchased by the twenty-kilo bag at a feed store an hour or so away.

It wasn't the goats' fault that my cheese was a failure. They were all good milkers and accepted us as their new masters, allowing us to put a bucket just behind their hind legs and then to squat down and squeeze the milk from their udders. The udders were as distinctive as the animals themselves, and we came to know the goats by the shape and color of their mammary glands and to learn the style and rhythm of milking that suited each. Some had long, dangling udders with teats that seemed part of the udder itself. These could be milked in one long, smooth squeeze, the jets of milk going directly down into the bucket. Others had plump, round udders, with small teats pointing out to the sides. These were more difficult to milk, and I often lost a stream or two as I tried to angle the teat downward toward the bucket.

Donald and I usually milked together, in the morning and again in the evening. We clipped the goats by their collars to the manger, where we gave each a half-bowl serving of cracked barley, a grain notable for increasing milk production, but not digestible if left whole. After each goat was milked, we poured the bucket of milk through the double-lined filter set on top of the milk can. As soon as all the goats were milked, we took the can of filtered milk into the house, poured it into one of the white plastic tubs we had purchased in Lyon, and added rennet.

The first batches of cheese that I made were inedible: coarse and grainy, filled with air pockets, sour and bitter. Watching their progression from curds to cheese, I had suspected they would be no

good, but I kept hoping. It wasn't until the third day, when the cheese was supposed to be ready to eat and sell, that I admitted they were worthless. I took one to Mme. Rillier and asked what was wrong. She told me I had used too much rennet. I threw all the cheese on the compost pile.

With the next milking, I reduced the amount of rennet, using barely a drop for twenty or so liters of milk. I wrapped the plastic tubs of milk in heavy quilts to keep them warm during the curdling period, and I crossed my fingers. When I looked at them twenty-four hours later, the milk had not separated into curds and whey, but only thickened. When I tried to scoop it into the molds, it ran out the holes. It seemed I hadn't used enough rennet. I left it another twelve hours, hoping it would curdle with more time, but it didn't. It, too, went on the compost pile.

Finally, after more than a week of trying each day to get the amount of rennet correct and to keep the curdling milk warm in the basins, I had produced only inedible, unsalable cheeses. I tried to keep my mounting sense of desperation hidden from Donald and Ethel, and I kept trying. Finally, one day I unmolded a batch of cheese that felt different. Each round, dimpled with marks from the mold, felt firm and heavy in my hand as I turned it out for the final time. They were all sparkling white and looked appetizing, unlike my earlier efforts, which had produced gray to yellowish cheese with cratered surfaces, sometimes slippery with the beginning of pink mold.

I put one of the pristine cheeses on a plate and cut a V-shaped wedge. The interior was solid and smooth, creamy, and white, with not a hint of the air pockets I had come to dread. I tasted it. It was soft, slightly tangy, and very, very good. I called Donald and Ethel, who took tastes, and we danced around the room, holding hands. We had done it! We had made old-fashioned farmstead goat cheese! I got out our labels that had arrived a month before from Lyon where we had ordered them. They were maroon foil, with a gold-embossed border and gold lettering with Donald's name, our address, and the fat content of the cheese, as required by law. At last, I had gotten the rennet and the curdling temperatures right and had made cheese, really good cheese. Everyone had been right. It was a simple process—but mastering it had been difficult.

I put a label on every one of the two dozen cheeses and carefully placed the disks in a shallow wooden crate lined with food-grade waxed paper. That afternoon I took them around to various people I knew for tasting. Mme. Lacroste and her mother declared them perfect, and each bought two. Georgette and Denys Fine swore they were as good as any they had ever tasted and bought three, one for Georgette's parents who were visiting. Georgette took me up the road to meet Françoise Lamy, who bought two as well, and then to Marie and Marcel Palazolli's, just across the road from the Lamys. Marie and Marcel were not there, but the door was open, and Georgette took me inside and told me to leave two cheeses for them. They'd pay me later; not to worry.

FÊTE DES OLIVES

The olive tree, one of Provence's most potent symbols, came 2,500 years ago with the Phoenicians who colonized Marseille. Now groves of shimmering silver olive trees are part of the landscape, from the terraced cliffs rising about the Roya River in the Alpes Maritimes in the back country of Nice to the rolling hills of the department of the Var to the famous Vallée des Baux, not far from St. Remy and Arles.

Olive trees are valued for their fruit, which are preserved for the table or pressed to release unctuous oil. As you might imagine, different regions of Provence have different styles of olive oil. The olive oil's characteristics also depend upon the variety of the olive and the maturity of the fruit at harvest. Along the coast, near Nice, the olives are pressed when black, nearly fully mature, to render a soft, delicate oil. In the area around the Bouche de Rhône, the olives are pressed when still partially green, and the oils have a more piquant flavor.

The Vallée des Baux, known for the high quality of its olive oil, is also known for the special table olives that are produced there, Olives Vertes Cassées, which are now an AOC (Appellation d'Origin Protegée) protected product. The olives are harvested in late September, cracked and then cured for a short period of time in brine with fennel, wild thyme, and bay leaves. These are the olives that mark the beginning of the new season.

Not surprisingly, in Provence, various fêtes celebrate olives, and one of the most colorful is the Fête des Olives Vertes held the third weekend of September in Mouriès, a village in the Vallée des Baux, which has three active olive oil mills. Like many fêtes, there is a fair in the main village square where vendors offer olives and olive-related wares such as oils, soaps, baked goods, olive-themed ceramics, olive wood creations, and even trees, but the Mouriès fête has some very special elements as well.

On Saturday, the first day of the fête, there is an olive cracking contest for anyone who wants to sign up. The task is this: crack open the flesh of as many green olives as you can in three minutes. The flesh must be only cracked open, and neither the flesh nor the pit crushed, as these are not suitable for making the finished olives. It is trickier than it sounds because the olive must be hit just so to

crack it open—too weak a blow will only bruise the fruit, while too hard a blow will crush it.

On the second day of the fête, after the blessing of the olives at Mass, a long parade weaves through the narrow streets of the village. To watch the parade is to witness a living tableau of what Provençal life was like one hundred or more years ago. In addition to the costumed drummers, fife players, prancing horses, and women dressed in elegant laces, there are costumed representatives of all the métiers, both old and current. Donkeys pull carts stocked with vegetables, farm workers push wheelbarrows loaded with green olives, traveling wooden wagons with hostelry supplies are pulled by a team of horses, and men lead donkeys laden with cans of milk. Groups of dancers swirl, with some of the dancers carrying beribboned arches of flowers over their heads while performing intricate steps.

Mixed in with the crowd are men and women, boys and girls, all dressed in the clothing that was common to the different classes of society during the late nineteenth and early twentieth century. Babies, with white piqued caps of the period tied snugly beneath their chins, are pushed in old-fashioned, authentic prams and poussettes, women stroll arm in arm with parasols, men in top hats walk chatting, while alongside them stroll workers in leather aprons.

After the parade is officially over, the streets remain full of costumed locals, and music seems to come from every corner. At noon or thereabout, there is an apéritif offered by the city in the square, followed by a "repas champêtre" or country-style community meal. While the dishes served may vary from year to year, you can be assured there will be a generous amount of olive oil incorporated into the meal.

Sautéed Garlic, Red Peppers, Chicories, Chard, and Spinach for White Cheddar Polenta

Serves 4

The first chard I ate was from my neighbor's garden. She later showed me how easy it was to cook it, and I devised serving it over polenta with cheese.

Polenta:
6 cups water
1½ teaspoons sea salt
1 cup polenta
2 tablespoons butter
4 ounces white cheddar cheese, grated

Greens:
1 bunch Swiss chard (10–12 ounces), ribs removed
1 bunch chicory or dandelion greens (8–10 ounces), stems removed
1 bunch spinach (10–12 ounces), trimmed
3 red, gold, or orange bell peppers or other sweet peppers
2 tablespoons extra-virgin olive oil
2 cloves garlic, chopped

Pour the water into a saucepan, add one teaspoon of the salt, and bring it to a boil over high heat. Add the polenta in a very slow, steady stream, stirring as you pour. Reduce the heat and cook for 40–45 minutes, stirring frequently. The polenta is done when it pulls away slightly from the sides of the pan.

While the polenta is cooking, wash the greens carefully to remove any bits of sand or grit. With a sharp knife, cut the bunch of leaves lengthwise into 2 or 3 strips. Dry the greens thoroughly in a salad spinner or gather them up in a clean cloth and roll them dry.

Cut the peppers in half lengthwise and remove the seeds and ribs. Cut the halves lengthwise into thin slices.

Just before the polenta is ready, heat the olive oil in a large skillet and add the garlic and sweet peppers. Sauté for 2 or 3 minutes and then add the greens. Sprinkle with the remaining salt, reduce the heat, cover the pan, and cook for 3 or 4 minutes. The greens will steam and reduce considerably in volume. Remove the cover and continue cooking until the greens are limp but still retain their color—a few minutes.

When the polenta is done, stir in the butter, cheese, the remaining ½ teaspoon of salt, and pepper. Remove the pan from the heat and spread the polenta onto a warmed serving platter. Top it with the mixture of sautéed greens and peppers and serve at once.

Escargots with Pastis

Serves 4

During our sojourn in France, we were introduced to the age-old technique of gathering snails, feeding them on cornmeal and wild thyme for 2 weeks to cleanse them, then cooking them. However, it is easy to buy good quality canned snails, and that is what I use now.

8 ounces butter, at room temperature
2 tablespoons shallots, minced
3 cloves garlic, minced
2 teaspoons white wine
1 teaspoon pastis
1 handful flat-leaf parsley, minced
24 snails

In a bowl, combine butter with the shallots, the garlic, the white wine, the *pastis*, and the parsley. With a fork or the back of a wooden spoon, mash it all together and then refrigerate it overnight, covered to allow the flavors to develop.

When ready to cook the snails, preheat an oven to 400 degrees F. Put about a tablespoon of the butter in each of four 2-ounce ramekins. Add 6 snails to each and top each with another tablespoon of the butter. Place the ramekins on a baking sheet and then put the baking sheet into the oven. When the butter froths and bubbles and the snails are hot, about 8 minutes, remove and serve immediately with lots of crusty bread for dipping into the butter.

Fried Ravioli with Garlic-Spinach Filling

Makes about 20, serves 5 or 6

These ravioli, each as large as the palm of a hand, are sold in the markets of Digne and Forqualquier in Haute Provence. Some are filled with garlic-laden spinach, others with cheese and potato purée, and still others with seasoned lamb. All are lined up on floured boards and, on request, are dropped into a vat of hot oil, where they sizzle and puff to a golden brown. Removed with tongs and quickly drained, each is then wrapped in a paper napkin and handed over to the happy snacker.

This is my version, but without the deep-frying. Instead, the ravioli are cooked in a skillet in shallow oil. And, you can also purchase the raviolis and fry them, making this a short-cut dish.

For the Filling:
3 pounds spinach, carefully rinsed and tough stems removed
3 tablespoons unsalted butter
3 cloves garlic, minced
1 onion, chopped
1 teaspoon sea salt
1¼ teaspoons freshly ground pepper

For the Dough:
2 cups all-purpose flour
2 egg yolks
1 tablespoon extra-virgin olive oil
Canola oil or other light oil for frying

To make the filling, bring a large pot of salted water to a boil. Add the spinach and cook until tender but still bright green, 3 to 4 minutes. Drain and rinse under cold running water. With your hands, squeeze the liquid from the spinach until it is as dry as you can make it. Chop finely, using scissors or a sharp knife. Set aside. You should have about 4 cups.

In a skillet, melt the butter over medium heat. When it foams, add the onion and garlic and sauté until translucent, 2 to 3 minutes. Add the spinach, salt and pepper and cook, stirring often, until all the liquid has evaporated, about 5 minutes. Remove from the heat and set aside until ready to fill the ravioli.

The dough is easily made in a food processor. First put in the flour, followed by the egg yolks, olive oil, and salted water. Process until a sticky ball forms. Place the dough on a floured work surface and knead until the dough is elastic and will roll out easily, about 7 minutes. Loosely wrap the dough in plastic wrap or aluminum foil and let stand at room temperature for 30 minutes.

Divide the dough into 2 pieces. On a large, well-floured work surface, roll out 1 ball of dough into a rectangle 16 by 20 inches and about ¼ inch thick. (You can also use a pasta-making machine to roll out the dough. I use an Atlas manual model.) Visualize the sheet of dough as if it were divided into 4-inch squares. Place about 3 tablespoons of the filling in the center of each square, smoothing and spreading it out to within ½ inch of each of the sides. Roll out the remaining dough into a sheet of equal size and lay it over the first. With the edge of your hand, press the upper sheet onto the lower one, forming lines between the filling lumps to seal the edges of the ravioli. With a pastry cutter or a sharp knife, cut along each sealing line, dividing the filled dough into approximately 4-inch squares. Crimp the edges together.

The ravioli are now ready to cook. If, however, you want to wait several hours before cooking them, arrange them in a single layer, not touching, on a flour-dusted cloth or piece of waxed paper. Dust the ravioli well with flour and cover with another cloth or piece of waxed paper.

To cook, pour the oil into the skillet to a depth of ½ inch. Place over medium heat until a drop of water flicked onto the surface of the pan sizzles. Fry the ravioli a few at a time, being careful they do not touch. Cook for about 2 minutes on the first side, and a little less on the second. When golden brown, remove with tongs to paper towels to drain.

Keep the ravioli in a warm oven until all are ready, or serve as they are prepared, a few at a time.

My Cheeses Gain a Following

The last two cheeses from my first successful batch I took, at Georgette's insistence, to a country *auberge* of some repute. The couple who ran it were formidable. She was said to be a harridan, he a sweet and charming alcoholic.

It was four o'clock in the afternoon, after the lunch hour and, I thought, a good time to call. I walked up the rear steps that led to the restaurant kitchen, as Georgette had instructed me to do, and before I could knock, the door swung open.

"Yes? What do you want?" asked a tall woman with a curly topknot of orange hair and heavily mascaraed eyelashes, thrusting her face toward me.

"Georgette sent me. I'm the American with the goat's-milk cheese. She thought you'd like to try some."

"What about Georgette and cheese?" a male voice called from the background. A tall, thin man dressed in chef's whites came to the door. He looked at the box of cheeses I held and asked me to come in.

The woman shrugged her shoulders and stepped back. "*Entrez.*"

I entered, and there before me was a Provençal kitchen. It had heavy wooden ceiling beams, with hanging copper pots and pans of varying sizes. A fireplace was set in one wall, its embers still glowing. A long, black spit was operated by a series of weights and counterweights. Terra-cotta gratin dishes were stacked next to big soup pots, and shelves held a collection of Provençal plates and platters in green and ocher. The remains of a meal, theirs I assumed, was spread out on one end of a long, heavily scarred wooden table that ran nearly the length of the room. The other end held a brace of unplucked pheasants.

"Here. Put the cheeses here," the man said, offering me his hand. "I'm M. Duvivier; my wife, Mme. Duvivier." We all shook hands.

"Sit down; sit down," he gestured, putting a chair between the lunch remains and the pheasants. "Would you like coffee? We are just having some." I accepted, and we had some small talk before he said, "Now, let's sample the cheese."

He took a knife, and as I had done, cut a wedge, first for his wife, then for himself. They were quiet when they finished. My heart sank. If these people, experts of the *terroir*, *gastronomes*, didn't like my cheeses, I didn't know what I would do. I hated Georgette for sending me there. I could feel my chest tightening, a sure sign that tears were not far behind, and I got up to leave.

"Sublime. Truly sublime!" M. Duvivier cried. "How is it possible that an American could make such a French cheese? I'll take them all to start with, then we'll see. I'll age a few myself, have others fresh, yes, yes, local cheese. Wonderful!" He grabbed both my hands in his.

Mme. Duvivier smiled. "Yes, it's very good, my dear. Very good indeed. And if my husband likes it, it is a great compliment. He is very particular, you know. That is why people come here, from Paris even, to eat his food."

I left the cheeses with them, accepted the thirty-two francs fifty they gave me, and headed home, excited about telling Donald and Ethel the good news about our cheeses.

Soon I was selling our cheeses on a regular basis to the *auberge* and the local *épicerie,* and at the Saturday market in Barjols, and on Wednesdays in the square of a small village where I was the only vendor and people came out of their houses just for my cheese.

On market day, I got up at five to milk the goats and do my cheese work before packing my cheeses onto the racks stacked in the back of the *deux chevaux camionette*, our little bluish gray van, circa 1958. Once at the market, I set up the table at my designated location on the square and displayed my cheeses, putting a label on each before covering them with white plastic mesh to protect them from dirt and insects.

As people bought my cheeses, I wrapped them in parchment paper, took the money, and put it in a small metal box. I quickly had a following of customers, and as word got around that we had fresh goat's-milk cheese, people would even find their way to our house to buy them, sometimes a dozen cheeses at a time, making the bumpy journey over the dirt road and across the trickle of stream to get to us.

I Become Pregnant, and
We Move to La Cellule

We stayed in the house by the forest with the goats, and soon a pig, through the spring and summer, and into early fall. But, especially when I became pregnant, it was clear that we couldn't live there through the winter. Rain sometimes made the road impassable, the fireplace didn't provide enough heat, and with the shortening days and no electricity, nightfall came quickly.

Our friends Denys and Georgette Fine offered to rent us a place on their property, a house of three small rooms—a kitchen and two bedrooms—that they called *la cellule*, the cell. Their property had once been a tile factory, and they had created the little house from the ruins of the vats where the clay had been stored, eventually living there with their two sons while restoring the main house next door. We decided to accept. We could continue to keep the goats and the pig where they were, going back and forth across the valley to tend them.

I loved my new kitchen. It was cozy, with a woodstove, a glossy red-tiled counter fitted with the usual two-burner cooktop, a round limestone sink with running water, and a built-in table with artistically sculpted white plaster benches on three sides. A large cupboard, partially screened in the rear to let in cold air, served first as our refrigerator and later as a cheese-curing cupboard. There was even a large, outdoor summer kitchen with an ivy-covered roof. A red-tiled pathway ran the length of the house and gave onto a broad yard bordered with bay laurel trees, rosemary, and the remnants of a stone wall.

As winter began to descend, and the baby's due date approached, I started making thick vegetable soups and stews, simmering them on the back of the woodstove for hours at a time. Ethel, standing on top of a footstool, made her first pancakes using the cooktop. My kitchen was always fragrant with the wild thyme and rosemary I had gathered and hung from the rafters. At night, Donald read stories aloud to us as I cooked dinner and Ethel drew or played with her toy animals, our dog Tune curled at her feet. It was, at last, the beginning of home.

One Sunday, we were invited for an apéritif by the Brunos, a couple who had befriended us and took an interest in the goats and what we were doing. I brought them several of our fresh cheeses.

"Oh, thank you! Thank you!" M. Bruno said, unwrapping one and bringing it up to his nose, breathing deeply. "Ah, so sweet, so fresh. Bravo! You have done a wonderful job with your cheeses. *Ils sont les vrais fromages de chevre d'autrefois*—the real goat's-milk cheeses of the past."

I felt my face flush. Although he and many others had told me this before, each time I heard my cheeses praised made me feel proud of what we had done. It was an especially important compliment coming from him because he loved and appreciated good food and wine and was knowledgeable about their origins. He knew how to make goat's- and sheep's-milk cheeses, to cure meats, to slaughter and butcher, to

raise animals of all kinds, to choose the best fish and shellfish, and to make wine and *vin maison* and liqueurs. He also knew where to find wild asparagus and mushrooms. He was, like so many Provençal men I've met since, fascinated by local ingredients and food and how to cook them, and far more interested in talking about that than about his work. I never heard about what occupation M. Bruno pursued, other than his wife's references to his years in the Legion, and some apartment properties that were occasionally mentioned as a reason for needing to return to Marseille where they lived most of the year.

THE GRAND AÏOLI FÊTE

This is one of the great summer feasts of Provence. The occasion might be a Sunday midday gathering in the country for friends and family, or a local *fête du village*, or village festival, such as the one celebrating the Feast of the Assumption on August 15. Throughout the villages, one can spot flyers posted on the shutters and doors of local bakeries, grocery stores, and city halls advertising *un grand aïoli*, a feast centered around vast amounts of pungent aïoli, the garlic-mayonaisse of Provence, accompanied by summer vegetables and salt cod. The price of participation, and the times and prizes for the *boule* contests that will be held and where the tickets can be purchased are also noted on the flyers. The communal meal, held outside, is the crowning event of the two- to three-day celebration that includes a *bal*, or dance, the night before, and multiple *boule* tournaments. You have to pay in advance for the meal and to subscribe to the tournaments, so plan ahead. Usually a certain number of places are available, and once those are taken, no more are added. The affair for a small village might have room for three hundred people; larger villages can manage up to six hundred.

Although I prepare at-home *aïoli* parties, nothing quite compares to being part of a village *grand aïoli*. In the morning, long tables covered with white butcher paper are set out beneath the spreading sycamore trees of the town square. Down the center of the table march bottles of local wine, red and rosé mostly. A stand is set up to dispense *pastis* and other drinks; potato chips and olives are sometimes offered *gratis*, and by 11:30 the square begins to fill with women and children. The men, and some women, too, have been there since the morning for the *boule* matches.

The women arrive carrying baskets with the necessary plates, silverware, glasses, and napkins, as this is a bring-your-own-table-setting affair. The clank of the *boules* resounds in the background, and the aroma of the golden, garlicky mayonnaise, the *aïoli*, floats on the warm air.

By 12:30, everyone is seated, the wine is flowing, and volunteers are bustling about, dropping fistfuls of sliced, fresh, baguette on the tables. The village women have been cooking all morning, and now they carry cardboard boxes filled with boiled vegetables to the tables. One by one they file by, dropping onto each waiting plate a carrot or two, a boiled potato, a handful of green beans, a beet, a hard-cooked egg, a chunk of salt cod, and sometimes snails. They laugh as they refuse or acquiesce to pleas for more beans or another potato or egg. Others come behind, offering the aïoli, sometimes spooning it out directly from the mortars in which it was made. Usually there are two versions, one made with extra-virgin olive oil, which is quite pungent, and the other made with a vegetable oil, which is milder. I like to opt

for a little of each. As the happy revelers dip the first vegetable into the *aïoli* massed on their plates, a relative silence settles over the crowd, followed by the rolling sound of conversation and laughter. Strangers sit side by side with local residents and are welcomed, quickly becoming friends, at least for the moment, with their neighbors, all bonding over the celebratory meal. In the smaller villages, there might be entertainment by the locals, consisting of Provençal songs sung by the baker's wife, occasional jokes and stories, and accordion playing. In the larger venues the entertainment is more typically professional, but of the same genre. As the wine bottles empty, and the last crumbs of the pastries have been consumed, people begin to drift off for coffee, to play or watch the *boule* games that have started again, or to take ambling walks.

A Personal Aïoli Party

Serves 12

For the Aïoli:

6 to 10 cloves garlic, minced

Coarse sea salt

6 egg yokes, at room temperature

3 cups extra-virgin olive oil or half grapeseed oil and half extra-virgin olive oil,
  or only grapeseed oil

Freshly ground black pepper

24 boiling potatoes such as Yellow Finn, White Rose, or Yukon Gold

36 carrots

36 beets

5 to 6 pounds young, tender green beans

24 eggs

12 to 15 pieces of salt cod fillet, each about 6 ounces, desalted and poached.
  (see page 46 for technique)

In a small bowl, pound the garlic cloves and salt together with a pestle, and set aside. In a larger bowl, lightly beat the egg yokes with a whisk. Very, very slowly drizzle in about ½ teaspoon of the oil at a time, gently whisking it into the egg yokes. Repeat this until a thick emulsion has formed. This will begin to happen after about 6 teaspoons have been added. Once the emulsion is formed, whisk in about 1 teaspoon of olive oil at a time until all the oil is used. Gently stir in the garlic and salt mixture to make a paste. Season with pepper. You should have about 3 cups. Cover and refrigerate until serving.

Place the potatoes in a large pot and cover with water and 2 teaspoons salt. Bring to a boil, reduce the heat to medium, and cook until the potatoes are easily pierced with the tip of a sharp knife, about 25 minutes. Drain and set aside.

Peel or scrub the carrots, then cook them as you did the potatoes. The cooking time will be about 20 minutes. Drain and set aside.

Cut off any leafy tops from the beets, leaving ½ inch of the stem intact. Cook the beets as you did the potatoes but omit the salt. The cooking time will be longer, about 50 minutes to 1 hour. Drain the beets and set them aside to cool, then slip off the skins. Remember that the beets will stain red any food they touch.

Place the eggs in a large pot and add water to cover. Bring to a boil, cover with a lid, and turn off the heat. Let stand for 20 minutes. Drain and immerse in cold water to halt the cooking. Drain again.

To serve, place the vegetables, eggs, and salt cod on individual platters and set on the table along with the aïoli divided among several bowls.

Beef Daube with Dried Cèpes

Serves 6 to 8

Slow-simmering and full of rich flavor, the *daube*—a wine-based stew—is a classic dish that has many variations. In Provence *daubes* were once prepared in terra-cotta *dauberes*, then set to braise in a bed of coals in the rear or to the side of the chimney hearth where they would cook slowly over eight or ten hours. Today's *daubes* are prepared on the stovetop. The beef is marinated overnight, in local red wine and herbs, simmered the next day, and easily stored, its flavors ever deepening, to be served the day after.

Traditionally a piece of *roulade* is used to start off the sauté. The roulade, which is much like Italian pancetta, starts out flat, like bacon, but then is heavily peppered, salted, and packed with wild herbs, rolled up, and tied with string to cure. This brings a fine peppery flavor to the finished dish, which here is accomplished by the use of freshly ground black pepper and abundant herbs. Dried *cèpes*, *porcini* in Italian, bring a fulsome taste and further meatiness.

Daubes require the less tender cuts of beef that have gelatinous sinews and tendons that thicken and flavor the sauce. A fine, tender cut such as top sirloin will be wasted here, and its *daube* will be thin and pallid. Instead, choose boneless chuck or a combination of boneless chuck and beef shank, which become meltingly tender and flavorful with slow cooking and contribute fully to the sauce's construction.

The *daube* can be served directly from its pot, and its juices ladled over pasta. A wedge of Parmesan or of Gruyere and a hand grater passed from person to person at the table adds to the simplicity and casual sharing of the dish.

4 pounds boneless beef chuck roast or a combination of boneless chuck
   and beef shank
2 yellow onions
3 carrots
8 fresh thyme branches, each about six inches long
2 dried bay leaves
1 fresh rosemary branch, about 6 inches long
2 teaspoons sea salt
1½ tablespoons freshly ground black pepper (reduce to ½ tablespoon
   if using roulade)
4 cloves garlic
1 orange zest strip, 4 inches long by ½ inch wide

1 bottle (750 ml) dry red wine such as a Cote du Rhone, Zinfandel, or Syrah

⅓ cup minced roulade (pancetta) or 2 slices of bacon, minced

2 tablespoons all-purpose flour

2 ounces dried *cèpes*, some broken into 2 or 3 pieces, others left whole

1 cup water

Pappardelle pasta

¾ cup grated Parmesan cheese

Cut the beef chuck into 2- to 2½-inch squares. Trim off and discard any large pieces of fat. If using beef shank, cut the meat from the bone in pieces as large as possible. Place the meat in a large enamel, glass, earthenware, or other nonreactive bowl. Quarter one of the onions and add the pieces to the meat along with the carrots, thyme, bay leaves, rosemary, 1 teaspoon of the salt, half the pepper (remember to adjust if using roulade), 2 cloves of the garlic, and the orange zest. Pour the wine over all and turn to mix and immerse the ingredients. Cover and marinate in the refrigerator overnight.

To cook the *daube*, put the roulade or bacon in a heavy-bottomed casserole or Dutch oven large enough to hold the marinating mixture. Place over medium-low heat and cook, stirring occasionally, until the fat is released, about 5 minutes. Discard the crisped bits of *roulade* or bacon.

Dice the remaining onion, mince the remaining 2 garlic cloves, and add to the fat. Sauté over medium heat until translucent, 3 to 5 minutes. Remove with a slotted spoon and set aside.

Now drain the meat and reserve the marinade. Pat the meat as dry as possible. Do not be alarmed by its purplish color, as the wine is responsible. Add the meat to the pot a few pieces at a time and sauté for about 5 minutes, turning them once or twice. The meat will darken in color, but will not truly "brown." Remove the pieces with a slotted spoon and continue until all the meat has been sautéed. When the last of the meat pieces have been removed, add the flour and cook until it browns, stirring often. Raise the heat to high and slowly pour in the reserved marinade and all its ingredients. Deglaze the pan by scraping up any bits clinging to the bottom. Return the sautéed onion, garlic, meat, and any collected juices to the casserole or Dutch oven. Add the remaining 1 teaspoon salt and the remaining pepper, and bring almost to a

boil. Reduce the heat to very low, cover with a tight-fitting lid and simmer for one hour. While the meat is cooking, soak the mushrooms in the cup of hot water to soften them. Any grit will drop to the bottom of the water. When soft, remove the mushrooms with a slotted spoon and set aside. Drain the water through a fine mesh seive. Add the drained soaking water and the mushrooms to the simmering meat, cover again, and cook until the meat can be cut through with the edge of a spoon and the liquid has thickened, 1½ to 2 hours longer, for a total of 2½ to 3 hours.

Remove from the heat. Discard the carrots, herb branches, and onion quarters. Skim off some, but not all, of the fat, as some is necessary to coat the pasta.

Meanwhile, bring a large pot of salted water to a boil. Add the pasta, stir well, and cook until just tender, about 11 minutes. Drain.

Put the pasta in a warmed serving bowl and ladle some of the sauce from the *daube* over it, adding more salt and pepper if desired, and topping with ¼ cup of the Parmesan cheese and the parsley. Serve the *daube* directly from its cooking vessel, or from a serving bowl. Pass the remaining cheese at the table.

Cannelloni Filled with Beef *Daube*

Serves 6 to 8

At charcuteries and *traiteurs* in the area of Digne, Aups, and Puget-Theniers, ready-to-cook ravioli are sold stuffed with minced bits of the meat from a *daube*, mixed with a little spinach and some of the sauce from the *daube* to bind the ingredients. Restaurants list ravioli au *daube* on their menus, and at Saturday markets, sheets of twenty-four ravioli, dusted with flour, can be bought from the traveling *traiteur*. Farther south and west, the home-style preparation is cannelloni filled with the leftovers from the *daube* of the day before. Manicotti shells can be substituted for the cannelloni shells, but remember that the former are thicker than the latter and thus belie the lightness of this simple preparation.

1 pound spinach
2 tablespoons unsalted butter
2½ cups finely minced meat and some of the mushrooms, if possible, from leftover beef
  daube with dried *cèpes*
2 cups leftover *daube* sauce
24 cannelloni shells, each 4 inches long, or 12 manicotti shells, precooked according to
  package instructions and cooled

Thoroughly rinse the spinach and trim and discard the root ends. Plunge the spinach into boiling water for 1 minute, just until it turns limp but is still bright green. Remove and drain it, then rinse under cold water. With your hands, squeeze all the water from the spinach, then finely chop it by hand or in a food processor. Squeeze again after chopping.

Preheat an oven to 350 degrees F. Using 1½ tablespoons of the butter, grease an oven-to table baking dish large enough to hold all the cannelloni or manicotti in a single layer.

To prepare the filling combine the spinach, onion, and minced daube in a bowl. Add ²⁄₃ cup of the *daube* sauce, and mix together until well integrated and a soft paste is formed.

Using a knife, spoon, or your fingers, fill each cannelloni or manicotti shell with an equal amount of the beef mixture. Arrange the filled shells in the prepared dish. Pour the remaining 1⅓ cups *daube* sauce over the shells. Sprinkle evenly with the cheese. Cut the remaining ½ tablespoon butter into small pieces and use to dot the surface.

Bake until the shells are soft when pierced with the tines of a fork, the sauce is hot and bubbling, and the cheese is melted and slightly golden, 25 to 30 minutes. Serve hot directly from the baking dish.

We Are Given Instructions in Bouillabaisse Making

The Brunos' residence was a small two-story stone house with a red tile roof, set just below a narrow dirt road on a rise of land cut out from the *garrigue*-covered hillside, thick with scrub oak and juniper. Its plastered walls were painted pale chalk blue, a color popular in the 1930s, with wooden shutters stained dark brown and decorative iron grating on the lower windows and the window of the front door. It had no barns or lofts, just a recently built garage, so it was not a farmhouse. It was too small and modest to be a proper villa, and it was certainly not a manor house. I have never seen a house quite like it.

The front door opened directly into a square foyer with a massive, carved wooden staircase, more appropriate for a chateau than their small house, that twisted up to the second floor. The foyer was crowded with several small gilded tables whose spindly legs supported ebony statuary, carved boxes, pieces of jade and rose quartz, and a few large fossils. One table held a lamp with a maroon silk shade fringed in gold. Just behind the door was an elephant-leg umbrella stand, and, off to the side, a coatrack and a decorative cabinet. There was just room enough to move through the foyer to the stairs or to turn either right toward the bathroom door or left into the living room. The space felt a little claustrophobic, as did the rest of the house.

A round dining table, lit by a green glass chandelier, was in the corner of the living/dining room, which also held a large maroon tufted sofa, two overstuffed leather chairs, an Oriental rug on the tile floor, a curio cabinet in one corner topped with a record player, and a built-in armoire in another corner. The walls were devoted to bookshelves, oil and watercolor still lifes (M. Bruno's own work—and quite good), and a large clock. In the back of the living room was a doorway opening to the right, into the kitchen.

"This way; this way." M. Bruno led the way through the living room maze to the kitchen doorway.

"It's all in here. I picked it up this morning at the *quai des Belges*. The boats come in every morning there to unload their catch from the previous night. It's a wonderful place. The fishmongers are, well, they can be pretty coarse, but that's part of it. The important thing is the fish."

"Now, first of all," he continued, "I must tell you that it is very odd to be making bouillabaisse for only six of us." I thought it was nice that he included Ethel in the table count. The French think children are never too young to learn how to eat. "The minimum—the minimum—would normally be eight, but best of all, ten, twenty, forty—the more the better, because one of the secrets of a great bouillabaisse is the number and variety of the fish that are used."

He rolled up his sleeves and tied on a white apron, covering his hand-knit brown sweater-vest and ample midsection. He was about fifty at the time, and his brown hair had begun to thin and recede, showing more olive skin. His brown eyes twinkled as he talked, and whenever he smiled, a dimple appeared to the right of his chin. For

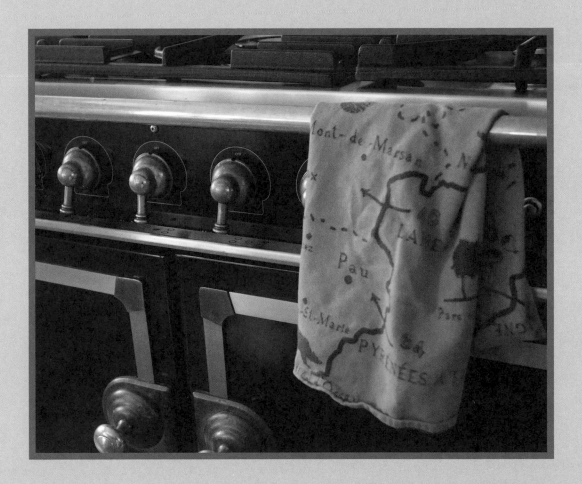

a Marseillais, known for the volubility of their arms and hands, his were, unlike his wife's, restrained. I wondered if it was the influence of his time spent in Asia, where he said he'd practiced Buddhism.

"Look. Here are the fish." He opened the metal cooler at his feet, and I saw a dozen or more whole fish laid on ice, plus a perforated metal container and some wet burlap bags. He tapped the container. "These are the *favouilles*, the little crabs. I have to keep them separate or else they'll gnaw on the fish."

The kitchen was tiny, with one small window above the composite granite sink, a waist-high refrigerator next to it, a stove against the rear wall, and a pantry. Pots and pans hung overhead. A curtain of traditional red Provençal fabric in tiny print gathered on a wire covered the open space and shelves beneath the sink and the countertop. I could have stretched out my arms in the middle of the kitchen and touched both hands, palms flat, to the opposing walls.

We stood hip to hip, as M. Bruno laid one fish after another onto a large, fennel-covered platter, discoursing on the culinary attributes and habitats of each fish while showing me the key signs of quality and freshness to look for. I was fascinated.

"Before we begin the fond, though, we need to season our fish. Here. Sprinkle this over them all. Be generous." The fond, I had learned, was the base of the soup. He handed me a wine bottle fitted with a stainless-steel spout. I had seen these before, so I knew it was olive oil, bought in bulk then bottled at home, just like wine (something Donald and I were just starting to do). I doused the fish while M. Bruno sprinkled them with sea salt, pepper, and saffron threads.

"And now, some fennel seeds." He rubbed a head of dried wild fennel between his fingers and the seeds scattered across the surface of the fish. I picked up some and did the same, releasing the sharp, sweet scent of licorice. He laid more fronds of fresh, bright green fennel, abundant now in late spring, across the fish. My nose tickled, there was so much fennel in the kitchen.

We spent another half an hour making the fond for the bouillabaisse. Ethel and Donald came in and out of the kitchen as we cooked. Ethel, intrigued especially by the fish on the platter, checked the fins and sharp teeth of the *rascasse*, comparing them to the delicately etched mouth of the *loup de mer*. "These are much prettier; don't you think, Mom? That one," she said, poking the side of *rascasse*, "looks scary and sharp." I thought of pulling sculpin from the seaweed beds off the rocks, taking them off the hooks, and throwing them back, carefully holding each one in a towel so I wouldn't get stabbed by the fins.

The fond began with olive oil, and we added leeks, onion, garlic, and tomatoes, along with freshly gathered wild thyme, sautéing everything in a large kettle until the kitchen was filled with the fragrance of the earth. Then the fish heads and bones from the cooler went into the pot along with the small crabs and the eel from the platter. I watched as the meat changed from opalescent to opaque, and the skulls began to emerge as the meat softened and fell away from the bones.

"Keep stirring while I get the *petits poissons*." Reaching into the cooler, M. Bruno pulled out a bag, opened it, and gently poured a rainbow of two or three dozen small fish, some no larger than my little finger, into the pot of hot oil and vegetables. Their red, orange-yellow, and olive-green hues quickly turned a uniform gray, their bright eyes sinking and becoming white with the heat.

"These little rockfish give the fond its richness. Like the *rascasse*, the *petits poissons* are essential." As he stirred, the fish gradually broke down and melted into the vegetables. Water and a length of dried orange peel were added, along with salt and pepper. As the stock simmered, the aroma subtly changed from the scent of the hills to that of the sea.

While the soup base simmered, M. Bruno led me through the steps of making the *rouille*, the garlicky, red pepper-based mayonnaise that we were to eat with the soup. We sliced a baguette and put the slices in the oven to dry (never grill them, he said), and then rubbed the rough, dry bread with garlic cloves.

Donald and Ethel had gone for a walk, looking for old Roman tiles. I stepped outside onto the terrace to visit Oliver, who was cooing and kicking his feet and waving his little arms in his baby chair while Mme. Bruno set the table under the chestnut tree, talking to him all the time. I walked to the edge of the terrace and looked out across the silent valley to the beginning of the Alps in the distance and thought how lucky I was to be experiencing this life. Then, after kissing Oliver, I went back into the kitchen.

The fond was finished, and we put it into a large, old-fashioned food mill, turning the handle until the crabs, fish heads, *petits poissons*, eel, herbs, vegetables, and liquid were transformed into a thick, brownish-gold soup. The fish bones and other debris were left behind in the mill and discarded. We strained the soup through a large, cone-shaped *chinois*, just to make sure there were no bones. As I held the *chinois* while M. Bruno poured, I was enveloped with the fragrance of the soup. I was getting hungry, and my mouth was watering in anticipation.

FEAST OF THE FISHERMEN: A GRAND FÊTE DE LA BOUILLABAISSE

The scent of saffron, fennel, and garlic wafts through the streets of the small fishing port of Le Brusc where every year on a Saturday or Sunday in June, more than 1,200 people sit down all together at long tables along the Quai St. Pierre to feast on bouillabaisse.

The Feast of the Fishermen: Fête de la Bouillabaisse, now more than twenty years old, is organized under the auspices of the *Comité de Liaison des Associations Bruscaines*, or CLAB, which joins together the approximately ten diverse associations and clubs of Le Brusc, such as the rugby club, the boule association, the football club, the wind-surf association, and the association of the parish of St. Pierre. The members of the associations do the cooking and the serving, and it is almost as much fun to watch the camaraderie and the competition among the groups as they cook as it is to eat the final results.

Huge cauldrons of simmering *bouilli*, the soup base, are watched over, stirred, sniffed, and tasted as the cooks ensure the *bouilli* is as perfect and as traditional as possible—a reflection of the natural world

they live in. The wild fennel and thyme come from the surrounding hillsides. The olive oil is from nearby olive mills, and the garlic and potatoes are from the new crops harvested earlier in the month from gardens and farms. Around each cauldron are stacked bins and baskets of Mediterranean fish and shellfish, fresh from the adjacent sea. *Rascasses*, *dorade*, *grondin*, monkfish, eels, mussels, and *favouilles*, the tiny crabs, all wait their turn to be added to the simmering soup, according to their size and type.

People arrive early to stake out their seats, to visit with friends and to survey the festive scene, or to see the various parades and activities that precede the meal. The port of Le Brusc, a part of town of Six-Fours-les-Plages, not far from Toulon, is sheltered, so even if the wind is blowing, which it often does, the community party is not disrupted. By noon, everyone is enjoying an apéritif of pastis or rosé wine from nearby Bandol or Cassis, celebrating in the increasingly festive atmosphere.

The bouillabaisse is served in the classical fashion, which is with the *bouilli* or soup first along with the *rouille* and the grilled bread. Bottles of wine and water are set out along the tables, and those are self serve, all included in the price of the meal.

After the soup, the platters of fish and shellfish arrive on the tables, with more *rouille* and bread. Bones, carcasses and shells begin to stack up as the meal, but not the festivities, draws to a close.

The celebration goes on, for those who make a full day (and evening) of the event, with *boule* matches, music, and some years a grand finale performance by a local dance troupe.

This fête sells out quickly, so people purchase their tickets early.

Poached Red Trout, Belgian Endive, and Watercress Salad

Serves 4

In winter, red, or salmon, trout are available in the fish markets, and I buy them often because I like how they combine a salmonlike taste and color with the naturally delicate flesh of trout. Browned in butter and then poached in tarragon-flavored white wine, these mild fish render a broth that forms part of the salad dressing.

Any greens can be used for the salad, but I think peppery watercress and crisp, slightly bitter Belgian endive go especially well with the citrus and tarragon flavors of the dressing.

1 bunch watercress
2 heads Belgian endive
1 tablespoon butter
1 tablespoon chopped shallots
1 whole red trout (about 1 pound) cleaned, or 2 or 3 red trout fillets
    (8 to 12 ounces total weight)
⅛ teaspoon sea salt plus more to taste
Freshly ground black pepper to taste
4 tablespoons fresh tarragon leaves
½ cup dry white wine
2 tablespoons fresh lemon juice
2 to 3 tablespoons extra-virgin olive oil (optional)

Choose 4 delicate clusters of watercress and reserve these to garnish the plates. Remove the leaves from the remaining watercress and set aside. Cut out the inverted V-shaped cores of the Belgian endives with a small, sharp knife. Separate the endive leaves and set aside 12 small, beautiful ones. Chop the remaining Belgian endive leaves and refrigerate, along with the watercress.

In a skillet large enough to hold the trout, melt the butter over medium heat. Add the shallots and sauté for 2 to 3 minutes. Season the trout with salt and pepper to taste. If using a whole fish, tuck 1 tablespoon of the tarragon leaves into the cavity; if using fillets, sprinkle the leaves on top. Put the trout into the pan (skin side down, if using fillets) and cook 2 to 3 minutes. If using a whole trout, turn and cook 2 to 3 minutes on the second side. Add ¼ cup of the wine, reduce the heat to low, and cover the pan. Cook until the fish is just done, 3 to 4 minutes. Remove the fish from the pan and set it aside while you prepare the dressing.

To the cooking juices that remain in the skillet, add the leftover 3 tablespoons tarragon leaves, the lemon juice, ⅛ teaspoon salt, and the remaining ¼ cup wine. Bring to a boil over medium-high heat and reduce by half. Taste and correct the seasoning. If the dressing seems too tart, add 2 to 3 tablespoons olive oil to smooth it out. Pour the dressing into a small bowl and set aside.

To serve the salad, flake the trout flesh into large pieces. Divide the chopped endive among 4 salad plates. Add an equal amount of watercress leaves and flaked trout to each plate. Garnish with the reserved watercress clusters and the whole endive leaves. Drizzle some of the dressing over each plate and serve at once.

Fava Beans and Salt Cod
in Green Garlic Cream

Serves 4

Green garlic, like green onions, are the immature stages of the vegetable before the bulbs have formed. Green garlic is available only in early to mid-spring, at the same time that fava beans are in season. The delicate flavors of the young garlic and the young favas make a fine match, here paired with salt cod. Poached fresh white fish would be good as well.

¾ pound salt cod
2 to 2½ pounds young to medium-mature fava beans
2 green garlic bulbs with stalks intact
⅔ cup heavy cream
4 cups water
2 teaspoons sea salt
1 teaspoon freshly ground black pepper
6 to 8 baguette slices, freshly toasted and rubbed with garlic

Rinse the salt cod under running water for 10 minutes. Soak the salt cod in cold water and cover overnight. The next morning, change the water and let the cod stand covered for 4 hours. Change the water again and let stand for another 2 hours. Rinse the cod under cold running water for 10 minutes. The cod will begin to plump up as it refreshes. Taste for saltiness. The actual length of time you will need to soak the cod will depend upon how much salt was used when it was cured. When desalted, the taste will be mild and somewhat sweet. Set aside until ready to cook.

Shell the fava beans. Bring a saucepan filled with water to a boil and add the fava beans. Boil for 1 minute, drain, and when cool enough to handle, slip the skins from the beans. You should have about 1 cup if you have used 2 pounds of unshelled beans. Set aside.

Cut each garlic stalk into four 1-inch-long pieces, starting from the bulb root end. Discard the leafy green upper ends. Pour the cream into the saucepan, add the green garlic, and let stand until ready to cook. The cream should be heated at the same time as the favas are being cooked.

Put the favas in water in a saucepan with 1 teaspoon of the salt. Place over medium-high heat and bring to a boil. Reduce the heat to low and simmer, uncovered, until the favas are tender, 6 to 12 minutes, depending upon the maturity of the beans. They should be bright green, tender, and neither crunchy nor mushy. Remove from the heat and drain. Return to the saucepan, freshen, and cover to keep warm.

Put the soaked cod in a shallow casserole or frying pan and add water to cover. Bring to a boil and reduce the heat to low. Cook just until the fish flakes when poked with a fork, 3 to 4 minutes. Remove from the water and when cool enough to handle, separate into flakes. Keep warm while you finish the cream.

Place the saucepan containing the cream and the garlic over medium-high heat and simmer, uncovered, for 10 minutes. Increase the heat to high, add the remaining 1 teaspoon salt and the pepper, and cook until the cream is reduced by about half and has thickened. Scoop out and discard the garlic.

Pour the garlic cream onto a warmed plate, add the fava beans, and scatter the beans with the warm poached salt cod. Serve immediately with baguette toasts.

Tomatoes Provençal

Serves 4

Platters of these appear on Provençal tables several times a week during summer, and they are perfect carriers for the regional flavors of garlic, olive oil, and fresh herbs. They might be served as a first course or as an accompaniment to a main dish, hot from the oven or at room temperature.

6 or 7 medium-size tomatoes, halved crosswise
3 cloves garlic, minced
A pinch of thyme
2 tablespoons minced fresh flat-leaf parsley
⅓ cup fine dried bread crumbs
1½ teaspoons sea salt
2 teaspoons freshly ground black pepper
¼ cup extra-virgin olive oil
3 tablespoons grated Parmesan cheese (optional)

Preheat a broiler. Place the tomato halves in a flameproof baking dish just large enough to hold them snugly. Sprinkle each half evenly with the garlic, thyme, parsley, bread crumbs, salt, and pepper, and then drizzle with the olive oil. If desired, top with the Parmesan cheese.

Place the dish under the broiler about 6 to 8 inches from the heat and broil until the tomatoes begin to soften and the topping browns, 8 to 10 minutes. Serve immediately or let cool.

The Secret Is in the Boiling

When we finished straining, we put the soup into a large, clean pot, reserving one cup to which we added a pinch of saffron threads. My teacher set the flame to simmer before pouring *pastis* for everyone. Donald and Ethel had returned by then with a bag full of finds, which M. Bruno exclaimed over and promised to peruse in detail after lunch. He passed around a plate of toasts with pâté, and I ate several while he continued to talk about bouillabaisse.

"The secret, the truth of the bouillabaisse, is in the boiling. The olive oil makes a liaison with the broth, and the fish are roughly handled by the boil, giving them a raggedy look. If the fish are not a little ragged, the bouillabaisse was not made correctly." He smiled and wagged his finger at me. "Remember that the next time you have it at a restaurant."

As we sipped our *pastis*, M. Bruno stirred the reserved cup of soup, now golden with dissolved saffron, into the simmering pot, then slid in the firm-fleshed fish, which must be cooked first, checking his watch. The soup, now on high heat, boiled over the top of the fish, and I watched in fascination as the skins broke slightly and whole chunks began to flake as they went from raw to cooked. When exactly twenty minutes had passed, he added the more delicate St-Pierre and the red mullets. These he cooked for six minutes.

"Ah," he smiled, "smell that." He was leaning over the pot, fanning the rising steam toward his nostrils. "There is nothing like a good bouillabaisse. Nothing." Donald and I copied him, sweeping our hands over the soup to bring us the aroma of the sea, made fragrant with saffron and orange. Ethel insisted on being lifted up so she too could wave her hand over the steaming soup, sampling it on the air.

M. Bruno gently removed the whole fish and chunks of monkfish to a platter. He ladled the soup into a tureen and set both on the table, which was already holding baskets of warm bread and bowls of *rouille*. M. Bruno instructed us to put a piece of bread into each of our shallow rimmed soup plates, and then ladled some of the soup over it. We helped ourselves to the spicy *rouille* that he passed, spooning it onto the softening bread. M. Bruno told us to eat while he filleted the fish, but first he filled our wineglasses with *vin blanc de Cassis*, the crisp white wine that comes from just east of Marseille.

What a taste! The bread rapidly became soft enough to cut off bites with a spoon, allowing me to dredge it in the *rouille* and the thick, intensely flavored soup. The explosion of flavors and textures was unforgettable. With each spoonful, the combination became better, and I kept thinking, "How is it possible that this elixir was made with fish heads and bones, small crabs, and fish almost too small to identify?" Soon my bowl was empty, and as I looked around, I saw the other bowls were empty as well. It was time for the fish.

When our host finished his tableside display of the deftest boning I have ever seen, he offered us the fish, serving us some of each, and then ladled more soup into our bowls, again passing the *rouille* and bread. Each fish had its distinct taste and texture, contributing to the wonder of the bouillabaisse.

"*Très, très bon, cheri*," exclaimed Mme. Bruno. "The fish are perfectly cooked, just the way your father would have done it. *Bravo!*" We chimed in with our compliments as well. Even though we had nothing to compare it to, we were sure we were eating the true Marseille bouillabaisse.

A Little History

The *quai de Belges*, bordering Marseille's Vieux Port, is still the place to buy the freshest fish and shellfish right off the fishing boats. Many boats that pull up to the *quai* are registered in Marseille, indicated by the letters "MA" following the registration numbers lettered on the sides. A vast number of them are owned by families who have been fishing here for generations. Knowledge of the secret places where the rocky shorelines shelter the *rascasse* and eels, the exact locations and fathoms for St-Pierre and *dorade*, and which stretches of sandy open spaces along the bottom hold the flatfish, has been passed down from father to son.

Marseille has been an important port ever since it was founded in the sixth century B.C. It is at the crossroads of Europe, Asia, and Africa, and through it at one time flowed all the foodstuffs and goods of the known world. Pilgrims set sail from here to the Holy Land and immigrants arrived here from France's once-extensive colonies. The flavor and taste of the city's exotic history come together in bouilla-baisse, its most famous dish.

Like all traditional dishes, bouillabaisse is saturated with lore and history. Every family, every port, and every neighborhood along the coast between Marseille and Toulon prepares a version. There is even a Marseillais legend that says Venus fed it to her husband, Vulcan, so that, once satiated, he would sleep while she carried on a dalliance with Mars. According to some stories, the soup was brought to Marseille by Greek mariners from Phocaea, in Asia Minor, who founded the city. These fishermen, and those who followed over the centuries, were purported to have boiled the leftover, unsalable, even spoiled bits of their catch in seawater. Scholars, however, have found no mention in historical documents that would substantiate this tale, and maintain that because the water of the Mediterranean is so salty, such a soup would be unpalatable, if not inedible.

The name *bouillabaisse* is thought to have originated from *bouillir*, which means "to boil," and *abaisser*, "to turn down." *Abaisser* also means, in culinary usage, "to reduce," which make sense in this context, because as the soup boils, it reduces. Although the primary meaning of *abaisser* is "to lower," the heat must be kept on high not only to reduce the contents but to create the essential liaison of olive oil and broth that, along with impeccably fresh fish and saffron, defines a good bouillabaisse.

Travelers in the 1800s, including Mark Twain, Émile Zola, and Gustave Flaubert, mentioned bouillabaisse when describing their sojourns in Marseille, as did the famous French gastronome Curnonsky, who called it *soupe d'or*, or golden soup, and raved about its essence and flavors.

By the mid-1800s, Marseille and the Côte d'Azur had been discovered by the rich, and fancy hotels and restaurants vied with one another for fame and for the customers who were passing through their cities. During this period, the golden soup as it is now classically made emerged, flavored not only with olive oil and garlic, but also with saffron, fennel, orange peel, onion, tomatoes, and aromatics.

The bouillabaisse with which most of us are familiar—a clear, sparkling broth laced with chunks of white fish, shrimp, mussels, and even scallops and lobster—has little in common with the bouillabaisse one finds in the best of the coastal restaurants from Nice to Marseille. A *Charte de la Bouillabaisse*, created in 1980 and signed by eleven restaurants, most of them in Marseille, states the ingredients and the method of preparing and serving a "true" bouillabaisse. This came about because an increasing number of dishes being served as bouillabaisse strayed far from the original version, endangering the very nature of the soup. The charter allows more flexibility than M. Bruno would have permitted: It acknowledges that shellfish can be added, as can potatoes, and that aïoli can be served as well as *rouille*. For the rest of the ingredients and the style of service, M. Bruno's version would have fit exactly the parameters for a true bouillabaisse.

Bouillabaisse

Serves 8

I start with making my own fish stock, like M. Bruno taught me, but you could skip this and purchase a good quality, ready-made stock.

The Fish Stock:
2 tablespoons extra virgin olive oil
1 large yellow onion, quartered
2 cloves garlic, crushed or sliced
2 carrots, each cut into 3 or 4 pieces
2 leeks, whites and pale greens only, cut into several pieces
5 pounds non-oily fish heads (make sure the gills are removed) and fish carcasses
3 or 4 sprigs Italian parsley
3 or 4 sprigs fresh thyme
1 bay leaf
8 peppercorns
2 cups dry white wine
6 to 8 cups water

In a Dutch oven or small stockpot, heat the olive oil over medium-high heat. When hot, add the onion, garlic, carrots, and leek whites and sauté, stirring, until limp, 2 to 3 minutes. Add fish heads and carcasses and cook, stirring, until they begin to turn opaque, about 3 minutes. Add the leek greens, parsley, thyme, bay leaf, peppercorns, and the wine and water. Bring to a boil, then reduce the heat to low, cover, and simmer about 30 minutes. Remove and strain through a chinois or a colander lined with cheesecloth. The stock can be made the day before, or up to 3 months ahead and frozen. If frozen, thaw before using.

The Toasts and Rouille:
Classically, the bread is air-dried (not toasted, not drizzled with olive oil) and just rubbed with garlic. The *rouille* is akin to *aïoli* thickened with bread and seasoned with spicy chiles.

3 dried cayenne or bird's eye chiles, seeded and chopped
5 cloves garlic
½ teaspoon coarse sea salt
1½ tablespoons dried bread crumbs
3 egg yolks
½ to ⅓ cup extra-virgin olive oil
1 baguette, cut on the diagonal into ¼-inch thick slices

To make the *rouille*, combine the chiles, garlic, and sea salt in a mortar and crush them with a pestle to form a paste. Alternatively, crush with the tines of a fork. Add bread crumbs and mix. Add the yolks and mix again until well blended. At this point, if the mortar is not large enough, remove the paste to a bowl.

Very slowly, drop by drop, stir in the olive oil using a whisk or an electric mixer, until the mixture thickens. Continue adding the oil in a thin stream, whisking or beating constantly, until a mayonnaise-like mixture forms. Set aside.

Place the baguette slices on a baking sheet and set in the sun to dry, or place in a 225 degrees F oven, turning once, until dry but not brown, about 20 minutes. Set aside.

For the Fish Marinade:
I love doing this part. The fresh fish against the green fennel, with its dash of saffron and drizzle of olive oil, is almost too beautiful to cook.

Fennel fronds from 2 bulbs of fennel (or, if you can find it, wild fennel fronds, ideally with flowering heads, loaded with pollen). Reserve after use for the soup.
1 fennel bulb, thinly sliced
1 pound firm white-fleshed fish such as halibut fillets, cut into 1-inch chunks
  ½ pound each of 3 to 4 different fish fillets such as petrale sole, red snapper, true cod, black cod, rockfish
2 whole fish such as black cod or snapper, cleaned and gills removed (these will need to be filleted before serving) each about 2 pounds (optional) or use more fillets and chunks
Pinch of saffron
2 tablespoons pastis or Pernod
1 teaspoon fennel seeds, toasted
½ teaspoon coarse sea salt
¼ cup extra virgin olive oil

Lay the fennel fronds and the fennel slices on a platter. Place the fish on the fennel in a single layer. Sprinkle them with the saffron, *pastis* or Pernod, fennel seeds, and salt, then drizzle the olive oil on top. Turn the fish and fennel several times to coat.

Let stand at room temperature, lightly covered, for 2 hours and up to 3 hours.

For the Soup:

⅓ cup organic extra virgin olive oil

1 leek, white only, chopped

1 medium yellow onion, chopped

3 cloves garlic, chopped

3 large tomatoes, peeled and chopped

4 cups fish stock

1 cup dry white wine

1 dry bay leaf or 2 fresh

¼ teaspoon freshly ground black pepper

1 pound raw prawns, heads and tails intact

Boiling water as needed

In a large, wide pot, heat the olive oil over medium-high heat. When it is hot, add the leek and onion and sauté until translucent, about 2 minutes. Add the garlic, then the fennel slices from the marinade. Sauté until the garlic is soft, another 1 to 2 minutes. Add the tomatoes and their juices, the fish stock, wine, bay leaf, and pepper. Remove the fish from the platter and set aside. Discard the fennel stalks from the platter, and scrape the remaining marinade into the broth. Stir and bring to a boil. When boiling, reduce the heat, cover, and simmer until the fennel slices have almost melted into the broth, about 30 minutes.

Increase the heat and bring the soup to a rolling boil.

Lay in the halibut and any other thick pieces of fish (and whole fish if you are using any). Add boiling water to cover. Cook 10 minutes. Add the thinner fish fillets, pushing them gently into the stock, adding more water if needed, and cook just until opaque, about 2 minutes. The fish will be raggedy and rough looking from the boiling, but this is what you want.

Remove the cooked fish gently to a platter and cover to keep warm. Add the prawns to the soup. Cook the prawns until opaque, about 2 minutes. Remove these and add them to the platter of fish. Remove the whole fish, fillet them, and return them to the platter. Bathe the platter of fish with a ladle of the soup. Keep warm.

Remove the bay leaf and thyme from the soup and discard them. Reheat the soup if necessary.

To Serve:

To serve, bring the garlic-rubbed bread and *rouille* to the table, instructing your guests to put a piece of bread in their soup bowl and top it will a dollop of *rouille*. Bring the soup to the table and ladle some into each bowl. Once everyone has finished the first course, bring out the platter of fish. Give everyone a bit of each kind of fish, drizzling the serving with a bit of the soup, and passing the *rouille*.

Green Olive and Almond Tapenade

Makes about 2 cups

The first green olives of the year are prepared in August to eat in September, the same time as the almond harvest, making this a seasonal spread that can nonetheless be made throughout the rest of the year. The nuts can turn rancid, however, so this tapenade doesn't store very well. The flavor is of olives and nuts, but if you desire, 5 or 6 anchovy fillets may be added as well. It makes a fine spread on its own or may be used as a sauce for fish or meat.

½ pound not-too-salty, brine-cured green olives, drained
1 cup blanched whole almonds
1 teaspoon minced fresh thyme
2 teaspoons fresh lemon juice
1 to 2 tablespoons extra virgin olive oil
2 teaspoons capers

Break open the olives by pressing on them with the back of a wooden spoon and remove the pits. Put the olives, almonds, thyme, lemon juice, olive oil, and capers in a blender and process until a paste has formed. (If you prefer, make the tapenade in the traditional way using a mortar and pestle.) Use the tapenade immediately or put it in a covered jar and store it in the refrigerator, where it will keep for up to two weeks.

Charentais Melons with Port

Serves 4

Every summer an argument arises at tables all over France about whether or not filling the cavity of a Charentais melon with port or another fortified wine ruins or enhances the flavor of the melon. In my experience, any Charentais melon or very good cantaloupe, if it is a fraction less than perfectly ripe, is delicious with port or with another vin doux. If, on the other hand, you have that rare and wonderful treat, a perfectly ripe melon, serve it *au naturel.*

2 Charentais melons or cantaloupes at room temperature
About 1 cup port wine

Cut the melons in half and scoop out and discard the seeds from the cavities. Put each half on a pretty plate, and fill the cavity to just below the brim with the port. Serve immediately.

Serve either as a dessert or as a first course.

I Go to a Party

Long after Ethel and Oliver were grown, and the bouillabaisse lesson with the Brunos a distant memory, I was teaching cooking classes in Provence and was invited to a bouillabaise party. Two brothers, both commercial fisherman, bought the big farmhouse at the bottom of my road and divided it into two adjoining living quarters. It had belonged to one of their uncles, so they had often been visitors to the house and were familiar with most of the villagers and their extended families and friends.

Once a year in the fall, they put on a semiprivate bouillabaisse feast, inviting eighty to a hundred people and charging everyone approximately twenty euros, just enough to cover their costs. The event includes apéritifs, hors d'oeuvres, bouillabaisse served correctly—according to the charter, in two courses—and a dessert. I discovered the event when a friend invited me to make up her party of six. I had just finished four week-long sessions of classes, and I looked forward to doing something different. The weather was still warm, as it so often is in late September, but the evenings could be chilly, so I brought along a wool shawl to wear over my long black linen sundress, because I knew we'd be eating outside until late.

I arrived just before 7:30, not wanting to be too early, just in case no one I knew was there yet. The road on either side of the brothers' house was already jammed with cars, and one of their wheat fields, now free of crop, had been turned into a parking lot for the night and it was also packed. Floodlights mounted on the edge of the farmhouse roof illuminated the scene below, where rows of tables dressed in white butcher's paper were ready for the guests. Old-time farmers and full-time residents mingled with the European and French urbanites who had bought second homes in the area. Everyone was wearing versions of summer finery and milling around the apéritif table where two of the most handsome men in the village, both masons with prematurely gray hair, dark brown eyes, weathered skin, and muscled forearms, were pouring a choice of *pastis*, rosé, or Coca-Cola. Voices rose and fell on the air, cicadas clicked in the background, and the scent of garlic cooking in olive oil came from the depths of the garage under the house.

I immediately saw my friend Yvonne, waving me to her table. She leapt up and kissed me on both cheeks, then introduced me to her friends who were visiting from Germany. Everyone brings their own tableware to these affairs, and Yvonne's was Rosenthal white china—huge soup bowls that were mostly rim, the kind you see in Michelin-starred restaurants. She also had flatware acquired on a recent trip to Thailand, crystal wineglasses, and heavy dark-orange linen napkins. Down the table, I could see a wide variety of tableware glittering in the light. By contrast, the apéritifs were in plastic glasses, and the hors d'oeuvres, which were peanuts, potato chips, and bite-size squares of *pissaladiere*, caramelized onion flat bread, had been handed out on small paper napkins.

"Come on, let's go see them cook." Yvonne grabbed my hand. She was a successful stage actress in Germany and also an excellent cook, voraciously interested in all things culinary. We headed straight to the

garage, which a hundred years ago had probably housed carriages, but now held two huge wok-like pans, each more than a meter in diameter and steaming with a broth whose fragrance of hills and sea reminded me instantly of M. Bruno's little kitchen. The pots were set on large gas rings built into a cement-block base about hip height. The rims of the pots rose almost to my waist, making them a good level for tending. The garage was deep and dark in the corners, but on the closer walls I could see hanging the leftover trappings of rural life: padded leather donkey collars, sieves for separating the grain from the chaff, pitchforks and rakes of worked-smooth wood. Had we been in a restaurant they would have seemed kitschy attempts at authentic décor, but here, on an old family farm, they were a natural part of the setting, just like the rototiller and disc whose outlines I could see in the far corner.

Along one wall, under the pitchforks and rakes, were a dozen or more plastic bins filled with fish. The incandescent lights of the barn selectively reflected their bright eyes and glittering scales, creating an unlikely seascape deep in the barn. I could identify some of the fish: small, bright orange mullets, considered a delicacy; St-Pierre, easy to identify because of the thumbprint; fat chunks of monkfish, whose ugly heads I supposed had already gone into the soup base; a whole bin of the spiky, essential *rascasse*; and many more fish, black, greenish, bluish, and red, whose names I didn't know. More bins, filled with peeled potatoes, stood next to the fish. On a small table between two of the steaming pans were a ceramic canister of sea salt, a glass jar half full of saffron threads, a big basket of bay leaves and wild thyme, and two glasses of *pastis*. I stood a moment, inhaling the scent of the place, before Yvonne dragged me over to be introduced as the American who lived up the road.

FÊTE DES TRUFFLES

Black truffles, known as "black diamonds" because of the high prices they bring, abound in Provence. There the truffle markets start in late November and continue until the season is over, usually sometime in February. The truffles are sold on specific days at different markets throughout southeastern France, which now supplies 80 percent of the black truffles sold in France.

Truffles grow underground in association with host trees, primarily oaks but also hazelnut, pine, and linden trees. The spores of the truffles produce filaments that gradually elongate and attach themselves to the roots of the host. Then mychorrhizae are formed, which then invade the roots, creating the habitat for the delectable fungus. The aroma, which dogs and pigs can sniff out, even if the tuber or tubers are deep underground, is pungent, earthy, and almost animal-like. The tubers are roundish and lumpy with a rough pebbly skin. They can be as small as the tip of a finger or as large as grapefruit, but most are somewhere in between. If you cut open a truffle, you'll find solid, dense, grayish black flesh faintly veined with white.

Truffles can't be spotted from above ground, except in the case of very experienced eyes that can see either the faint brûle, or grassless space beneath a tree that indicates truffles, or truffle flies hovering over the brûle. Thus, pigs and dogs are used to sniff out the tubers. Some people own forest land where truffles are naturally produced, and where acorns from a good "truffle" tree are planted to hopefully create new truffle trees. In the last decades, trees inoculated with truffle spores are available and truffle plantations can now be spotted in the rocky, sparse landscapes of the parts of Provence where the oak trees thrive.

In addition to market days, many of the villages located in the truffle-hunting regions in the departments of the Alpes de Haute Provence, the Vaucluse, the Gard, and the Drôme have Fêtes des Truffes. These are weekend-long events held in mid to late January and into early February. Like other fêtes, they are announced with flyers tacked onto telephone poles, taped onto the windows of the bakeries, cafés, and bar-tabacs, as well as being announced in local and regional newspapers.

One of the most notable of the truffle fêtes is associated with L'association des trufficulteurs de Haute-Provence and is held in a different village in the Alpes d'Haute Provence toward the end of January or early February. For two days, the selected village becomes a truffle capital. Demonstrations are given of "cavage," the official term for hunting truffles, called *rabasse* in Provençal, with dogs and sometimes pigs, doing the searching. Numerous truffle products, from bottles of truffle oil to truffle salts, are for sale by vendors at stalls set up for the occasion. Cooking demonstrations and seminars may be scheduled, and there may even be a brouillade "cook-off" where individuals compete to make the best truffled scrambled eggs, the simplest and most classic way of serving truffles.

Best of all, there is a community-sponsored truffle lunch, where up to six hundred people are seated and served course after course of dishes featuring truffles. These are usually quite reasonable, in the range of 45 Euros, and wine is included, of course, and in my experience, it flows freely.

This menu at a recent Fête des Truffes in Mane, a small village near Forcalquier in the Alpes–de–Haute Provence, is a good example of what you might find at a truffle lunch: Cream of Butternut Squash Soup with Grated Truffles, Braised Veal with Truffled Celery Root Purée, Truffled Camembert with Mesclun salad and a dessert of Blancmange

with Almonds, Truffles, and Saffron-Spiced Pears. All was served at the Salle Polyvalente or village hall, which is quite a common location for truffle lunches associated with the fêtes.

I well remember the one I attended in a small village near Riez. The meal was preceded by a procession of the members of the Order of the Truffles dressed in medieval-looking black robes, bedecked with golden tassels and red ribbons. We followed the procession through the village to the square where the mayor spoke, and then an apéritif of wine and pastis was served. Everyone stood about and chatted, even thought it was a very cold January morning. By 12:30, all five hundred of us were seated at long tables in the Salle Polyvalente. The tables were lined with wine bottles, to which everyone helped themselves. Soon, dish after dish arrived, each perfumed with truffles, along with the occasional speech. Several hours later, fully satiated, we headed back into the village for a brisk, reviving walk in the cold and an espresso before leaving.

The meal itself is designed and catered by a regional star chef or caterer and seems worthy of a Michelin star. While they may not be served in the most refined and elegant venues—all-purpose community centers tend to be the norm—the quality of the food and the conviviality of the participants more than makes up for what the setting might lack. As with most other community fêtes in Provence, the tickets or subscriptions must be purchased in advance.

It is worth planning a trip to Provence in winter and scheduling one or more truffle fêtes into your itinerary. Just be sure to purchase your meal ticket or subscription in advance so you won't be disappointed.

Artichoke and Fava Barrigoule

Serves 6 to 8

This is a favorite springtime dish in Provence, when the gardens and markets of full of young, tender artichokes and fava beans.

2 tablespoons extra-virgin olive oil
2 tablespoons minced green garlic, about 3 stalks
8–12 artichokes, small to medium, trimmed and halved
2 pounds of favas, removed from pods, skins removed or left on
¼ cup dry white wine
¼ cup chicken broth
2 to 3 sprigs fresh thyme
Pepper to taste

Heat the olive oil in a frying pan or sauté pan with a lid. When it is hot, add the garlic and sauté. Add the artichokes and favas and continue to sauté briefly. Then add the white wine, scraping up any bits. If more liquid is needed, add the broth. Add the thyme and the pepper. Reduce the heat to low, cover and simmer until the artichokes are tender, about 15 minutes. Remove and let stand until ready to serve. Serve hot or at room temperature.

Pork Medallions and Green Olives Sauté

Serves 4 to 6

The olives and bay leaves blend together to season the meat, onions, and juices with a distinctive flavor in this savory dish that takes only moments to prepare. I like to serve it with creamy mashed potatoes on the side to mingle with the savory juices.

1½ tablespoons organic extra-virgin olive oil
1½ tablespoons unsalted butter
1½ yellow onions, coarsely chopped
2 fresh bay leaves, or 1 dried
24 brine-cured tart green or black olives, pitted
1½ pounds pork tenderloin, cut into 1-inch-thick slices
½ cup water

In a skillet, melt the olive oil with the butter over medium heat. When the butter foams, add the onions and sauté for about 1 minute. Add the bay leaves and the olives and sauté until the onions are translucent, another minute or two.

Raise the heat to medium-high and push the onions and olives to the side of the skillet. Add the pork slices and cook for a minute or two, without turning, until the meat has changed color nearly halfway through. Turn and cook for another minute or two, just until the pork is cooked through.

Add the water and deglaze the pan by scraping up any bits clinging to the bottom, turning the pork in the juices as you do so. Serve immediately.

The Dinner Arrives

The brothers, each armed with a long metal spoon, were tending the pots of simmering soup. We all agreed we had seen one another in passing and were happy to meet finally. Both wore short-sleeved cotton shirts and jeans. One was wearing a baseball cap backward. The other had brushed his thinning brown hair back from his forehead. Their faces were rosy from the steam and heat of the soup and glistened with a faint sheen of sweat. I asked how much fish was in the bins.

"Oh, forty or fifty kilos are left. We brought up more than a hundred kilos, including the *favouilles*, but a lot went into the fond here," he said, as he stirred.

"Did you catch them all?" I asked, watching the golden soup as it rhythmically bubbled up, collapsed back, and rose again. I could just see the propane flames beneath the black bottom of the pots and feel their hissing warmth. The crowd outside had stopped milling, and people were beginning to sit down.

"Oh, not all. Most of them. We made a few trades. We had more of the deepwater fish, like the St-Pierre, fewer of the shallow-water rockfish, so we traded with another fisherman. We're all pretty friendly."

A lighted doorway suddenly shone in the dark rear of the garage, framing a woman carrying a basin. She came toward us.

"Eh, Jean, the *rouille* is ready. Just needs a little more soup." She indicated the ladle on the wooden table with a nod of her head and held out the basin. The closest brother scooped up some soup, poured it into the basin, and then stirred it until the stiff peaks of the reddish gold *rouille* softened and smoothed.

"*Bonsoir*," she said smiling at me and Yvonne. "*C'est bon, n'est-ce pas?*"

We agreed that it was good, everything—the evening, the setting, the fish—all the time eyeing the basin of fragrant *rouille*, thinking that soon we would be slathering it on top of our dried bread, into the soup, on top of the fish.

"Go on, have a seat. We're ready to bring out the *rouille* and serve the soup."

We left the garage and hurried back to our seats just in time to get a piece of bread into our bowls before a woman approached our table, laughing and joking as she came down the row, spooning the thick *rouille* on top of the waiting bread. Someone else followed with soup.

Yvonne poured the red Vacqueyras she had brought from her cellar. I thought it was a little powerful for the soup, but she likes big red wines, and it tasted good as the evening began to chill. As we set upon the soup and drank the wine, voices rose with laughter, and I could feel a bond growing among us, created by the sheer joy of eating bouillabaisse, a dish that everyone, including me, had memories of.

My bread softened with the soup, the *rouille* melted into it, and with each bite I tasted the garlic, roasted red peppers, fennel, saffron, fish, crabs, and eel, no longer discrete but melding to form the taste and texture of the fond. We served ourselves more toast and took more *rouille* from the small bowls brought to the table, while women passed

behind us with pots of steaming soup, ladling more into our bowls if we asked. I had two servings, plus extra toast, and then the fish began to arrive.

The deep platters were heaped with chunks of monkfish and fillets of red mullet and sea bass, plus buttery potatoes, tinted gold by the soup's saffron. I remembered that Monsieur Bruno didn't put potatoes in his bouillabaisse, but had explained that the Toulonnais swear by the necessity of potatoes.

I found myself caught off-guard by the memories that the bouillabaisse evoked of my past life, when the children were little and life seemed simpler. I excused myself early, explaining to Yvonne that I was more tired than I had thought. I managed to extricate my car from the crowded field where I had parked, and drove up the road into the night.

Beef and Leek Stew

Serves 4

In this dish, the natural sweetness of the leeks is enhanced and intensified when the pan is deglazed with balsamic vinegar and the stew is simmered until the leeks have melted into a rich brown sauce. The meat becomes so tender that it is easily shredded with a fork.

2 tablespoons extra-virgin olive oil
1½ to 2 pounds boneless beef chuck roast, cut into 2-inch chunks
3 large leeks
2 tablespoons all-purpose flour
1 teaspoon sea salt
½ teaspoon freshly ground black pepper
¼ cup balsamic vinegar
3 to 4 cups water

Cut the leeks in half lengthwise, then cut them crosswise into ½-inch-thick slices. Include all but the final 2 or 3 inches of the green shaft.

Heat the olive oil in a heavy-bottomed flameproof casserole or skillet over medium-high heat. Add the beef and cook until browned, 8 to 10 minutes. Add all but ½ cup of the leeks to the beef and cook for 4 or 5 minutes, stirring often. Sprinkle the leeks and beef with flour, salt, and pepper and cook for another 3 to 4 minutes to brown the flour. Add the balsamic vinegar and deglaze the pan, scraping up any browned bits that cling to the bottom. Slowly add 2 cups of the water and bring it to a boil, continuing to stir. Reduce the heat and cover the pan. Simmer the stew until a thick sauce has formed and the meat can be cut with a fork, about 2 hours. Add additional water, a little at a time as needed, to keep the meat moist until ready to serve.

We Return to California but Always Come Back to Provence

We left Provence not long after Oliver was born, and for the first time in more than three years, Donald and I returned to Provence, able at last to take advantage of the long summer holiday afforded us now that we were teachers in California. Our first stop was Deny and Georgette Fine's house, whose small rental we had lived in when Oliver was born. They were expecting us for lunch, and before we could get out of the car, they ran out to greet us with hugs and kisses. Ethel remembered them and threw her arms around Georgette, but Oliver, who was a baby when we left, hung back, clasping his green Hulk doll. He had no memory of these people who were speaking a strange language and kissing him, or of the snug little house he was brought to as a newborn.

Once the greetings were over, I took Oliver by the hand and went down the tiled walkway past the yard where I had played with him on his blanket and hung his diapers, and I told him about when he was a baby at this house. Ethel ran ahead of us, pointing out scenes of interest, such as the spot where she had seen the rat in the outdoor kitchen; the place under the bay tree where our dog, Tune, had attacked and killed one of the Fines' guinea fowl; and the creek where, looking for frogs with a friend, she had gotten soaking wet on a winter's day.

The acacia tree was just as I remembered it, but taller. In early June the bunches of white flowers were beginning to fade and dry, past their prime for dipping in batter and frying for the beignets I used to make. The kitchen where I had cooked so many meals was sooty and needed repainting, but in my mind's eye I could still see the wild herbs and drying strings of *sanguin* mushrooms that I had hung in the corner near the woodstove when we had lived there.

Georgette called me back from my memories, shouting "*Á table!*" and Donald came to get us. The Fines' familiar round green metal table, slightly rusted, was covered with a white embroidered cloth, and places were set for the six of us under the Virginia creeper that shaded their stone terrace. Georgette brought out a plate of pristine red and white radishes tipped with a few green leaves that she had pulled that morning from the garden, a plate of butter, and a small dish of salt. I silently promised myself I would buy radish seeds to take back to California and plant in our backyard. Denys followed with a basket of fresh bread, still warm from the bakery's late-morning bake, a bottle of red wine, and a carafe of water.

I had brushed against the sage near the table when I sat down, and its pungent fragrance hung in the air as we ate our first course, the crunchy radishes spread with just enough butter to hold the sprinkled salt. The wine, dark red and fruity, came from Taradeau, a neighboring village whose wine cooperative had a good reputation. After three years in exile in the Northern California bedroom community where we now lived, I felt that I had come home.

The wine was perfect with the bread and radishes and went just as well with the hot, bubbling zucchini gratin that came next and the salad that followed. Denys brought out a second bottle to have with the cheese. Dessert was fresh figs.

It was the kind of meal that Provence is famous for and the reason, I think, that people travel to Provence, rent a house there, even buy a house and move, just to be part of the life of the Provençal table. Those long meals, composed of simple, fresh seasonal foods and local wines, savored under the cooling shade of sycamore or mulberry trees in warm weather and in front of a cozy fire in cold weather, are the essence of the good life, well lived.

We Celebrate Bastille Day at Midnight

One of my best memories of long summer meals was a meal that took place in a village square at midnight on Bastille Day, the French independence day named after the infamous prison whose fall symbolized the end of the French monarchy and the beginning of the French Republic. Like the Fourth of July in the United States, the occasion is marked by fireworks and varied celebrations, most of them including food.

My friend Pascal had a summer job doing masonry work in Entrecasteaux, and while working there met the owner of one of the small restaurants on the village square. She was putting on a special meal for Bastille Day—bottomless bowls of *soupe au pistou*, wine, and bread for twenty francs, children under twelve half price. It sounded like fun, so we all decided to go. I had heard about the village, and even though it was only twenty minutes away, I had never been to it.

That night at Entrecasteaux, we ate our fill of *soupe au pistou*. As soon as the communal bowl was empty, a waiter or waitress brought a full one, then another, on into the night. Full wine bottles kept replacing empty ones, and baskets of bread never ended. It was after midnight before the apple tart arrived, and by then Oliver was asleep, his head in my lap. It was just chilly enough to put on the sweater I had brought, and the cicadas were less insistent in the cooling night. The teenagers had taken over the cobbled streets now, setting off firecrackers, while the adults were starting to head home.

Soupe au Pistou

Serves 6 to 8

For the Soup:
1 tablespoon extra virgin olive oil
1 small onion, diced
1 carrot, peeled and diced
3 small potatoes, peeled and diced
1 medium zucchini, diced
2 cups vegetable or chicken broth
4 cups water
1 teaspoon sea salt
4 sprigs fresh thyme
4 sprigs fresh parsley
1 pound fresh cranberry beans, shelled
1 pound fresh butter beans, shelled or double the amount of fresh cranberry beans
½ pound haricot vert cut into 1-inch long pieces
½ cup broken spaghetti pieces

For the Pistou:
3 or 4 cloves garlic, peeled and coarsely chopped
¼ teaspoon coarse sea salt
1 packed cup fresh basil leaves
⅓ cup extra-virgin olive oil

For the Soup:
In a large saucepan or soup pot, heat the olive oil over medium-high heat. When it is hot, add the onion and sauté until translucent, 2 to 3 minutes. Add the carrot, potatoes, and zucchini and stir several times. Add the broth, water, salt, thyme, and parsley and bring to a boil. Reduce the heat to medium, cover, and cook until the carrots and potatoes are tender, 15 to 20 minutes. If both the cranberry and the butter beans are firm to the bite, add them both at the same time and cook another 15 minutes, or until nearly tender. Add the *haricot vert* and the broken spaghetti and cook until the spaghetti is tender, another 8 to 10 minutes. With the back of a fork, crush some of the potatoes and beans to thicken the soup.

For the Pistou:

Put the garlic and the salt in a mortar, and using the pestle, crush them together to make a paste. The rough edges of the salt crystals act like little knives and cut into the garlic. Alternatively use a bowl and wooden spoon. Add the basil leaves a little at a time, crushing them. Finally, add the olive oil in a thin stream, continuing to mix with the pestle until the mixture has thickened and taken on a green tint. Set aside.

To Serve:

Remove the thyme and parsley sprigs from the soup and taste it for seasoning, adding more salt and pepper if desired.

Pour the soup into a tureen or serving bowl and ladle in 2 tablespoons of the *pistou*. Serve the soup hot, with the remaining *pistou* on the side.

Rosemary Pasta with Black Olives and Carrots

Serves 4

This was a dish I fixed often when we were first living in Provence and short of money. The flavors of the dish are satisfying, and the ingredients exceptionally inexpensive.

3 tablespoons extra-virgin olive oil
1 tablespoon butter
3 cloves garlic, minced
½ yellow onion, chopped
1 to 2 carrots, peeled and cut into very thin slices
1 teaspoon sea salt
1 tablespoon freshly ground black pepper
1 teaspoon minced fresh rosemary
½ cup oil-cured black olives
10 ounces dried pasta, such as penne or mostaccioti
¼ cup grated Parmesan cheese (optional)

Bring a large pot of salted water to a boil. Meanwhile, in a skillet warm 2 tablespoons of the olive oil and the butter over medium heat. Add half the garlic, all the onion and carrots, and sauté until the carrots are easily pierced with the tines of a fork, 7 to 10 minutes. Add the remaining garlic, salt, half of the pepper, half of the rosemary, and the olives. Continue to sauté until the olives are plumped and the edges of the carrots are slightly golden, about 3 or 4 minutes.

While the vegetables are cooking, add the pasta to the boiling water, stir well, and cook until just tender. Drain.

Place the pasta in a warmed serving bowl and turn it with the remaining 1 tablespoon olive oil and the remaining pepper. Add the contents of the skillet, including the pan juices. Add the remaining rosemary and turn to mix all the ingredients. Adjust the salt. Top with the optional Parmesan cheese if desired. Serve hot.

Grilled Butterflied Leg of Lamb
with *Herbes de Provence*

Serves 8 to 10

An alternative to cooking a whole lamb leg in the oven is to ask the butcher to butterfly the leg, removing the bone and leaving the meat in a single piece that will lay flat. Studded with garlic and seasoned with salt, pepper, and herbs, the lamb cooks over a medium-hot fire in about half an hour. The thickness of the butterflied lamb varies from about 1 inch to 2 or 2½ inches, so a single leg can be well done, medium, or rare, offering something for all tastes.

1 leg of lamb, about 5 pounds before being boned and butterflied
Stems reserved from preparing herb mixture, plus several lavender stems if
   using fresh herbs
6 cloves garlic, cut into slivers
1 teaspoon sea salt
2 teaspoons freshly ground black pepper
½ cup mixed fresh thyme, winter savory, rosemary, and marjoram leaves, in about
   equal amounts, plus a few lavender blossoms or substitute 2 tablespoons dried
   Herbes de Provence

Prepare a charcoal or a wood fire in a grill.

Dry the leg of lamb, then rub it all over with the stripped herb stems. Using a sharp knife, make 20 to 25 slits about 1 inch deep (depth depends upon thickness of meat) all over the meat. Insert the garlic slivers into the slits. Rub the meat on both sides with the salt and pepper and sprinkle with the herbs, pressing them into the flesh with the palm of your hand.

When the coals are medium-hot, place the lamb on the grill rack about 8 inches above the fire and cook for about 30 minutes, or until an instant-read thermometer inserted into the thickest part of the leg registers 135 degrees F for medium rare or 145 degrees F for medium. Turn frequently, watching carefully so the meat does not burn.

Remove the lamb to a cutting board or platter and cover loosely with aluminum foil. Let stand for 10 minutes, then carve into thin slices.

A Summer Life

So began our first summer back in Provence, when I would start to learn what it was like to live there as a summer vacationer, as part of the community but without the daily, arduous work of keeping goats and pigs. My days would be filled with food and cooking, long meals with friends and my family, and discovering the world that was to be part of me for the rest of my life.

Our social life, like everyone else's, revolved around food. We lingered over lunches and dinners, went to the open markets where we met friends for an apéritif or coffee, took picnics to the beaches and lakes, and went to restaurants and community feasts. We steeped ourselves in the tastes of Provence—olive oil, wild herbs, fish, tomatoes, eggplants, zucchini, grilled lamb and sausages, fresh cheese, and fruit of every kind.

In memory, it seems I spent at least part of almost every day cooking with my neighbors Marie, Georgette, Pascal, or Françoise. We all lived on the same road, a narrow, sinuous lane set in a small valley of unfenced vineyards, grain and melon fields, fruit orchards, and olive groves, punctuated by Marcel's vast market garden. Our days were subject only to the rhythm of nature and the table. It was natural for us all to pick cherries and peaches together from Marie and Marcel's trees; to help Françoise with the vats of tomato sauce she made to feed her children and grandchildren who came to spend much of the summer with her and Robert, to barbecue with Georgette and Denys, or to make elaborate dishes, like stuffed breast of veal, with Pascal.

That summer, and all the summers and years to follow, I cooked mostly out of my neighbors' gardens and orchards, especially Marie and Marcel's, and as often as I could, in the fireplace. Marcel was, and still is, the best vegetable and fruit grower around. Even now, in his mid-seventies, he plants more vegetables than he and all his relatives and neighbors can possibly eat, or that he can sell at the morning markets he and Marie still faithfully attend, as much for the sociability as for the income.

A favorite summer dish was simply potatoes cooked with beans until the beans were falling-apart tender, seasoned with salt, pepper, and *sarriette*, the winter savory that grows wild in high places. We followed the seasons with Marcel's fruit, beginning with cherries in early June; moving on to apricots, peaches, plums, and melons; and, just before returning to California in late August, figs.

That first summer back in Provence, Marie also taught me how to cook some of her favorite dishes, including *petits farcis*. I taught this dish to the students who came to my cooking school, after first taking them to one of the open markets to meet Marie and Marcel and to buy the vegetables we needed.

Marcel is from Nice, and *petits farcis* are a summer specialty of that city, although they are found all over Provence. Marie had learned how to make them from Marcel's *Niçoise* aunt, and that was the method she taught me. She began by scooping out halves of small eggplants, round zucchini, sweet peppers, and tomatoes. She finely minced the pulp of the eggplant and zucchini and seeded and chopped the tomato flesh. These all went into a bowl with a mixture of sausage and slices of a day-old baguette soaked in and swelling with milk. The mixture was seasoned with finely minced onion and garlic, parsley, thyme, salt and pepper, and bound together with an egg or two, then mounded into the vegetable shells.

Marie explained to me that now she cooks the *petits farcis* in her oven, but before she had an oven, she cooked them on top of the stove.

"I still do it that way sometimes. They get a crunchier crust," she told me one day as she poured a thin film of olive oil over the bottom of a large frying pan. She placed the stuffed vegetables in the oil, stuffing-side up, and cooked them gently for about ten minutes. "Now watch. This is Tatie's trick." Using a spatula and with a little help from her fingers, she turned the stuffed vegetables and gently cooked them until the stuffing was browned, something I would never have thought of doing. She turned them again, covered them with a lid, and cooked them another twenty minutes or so. The tomatoes were done a little sooner, so she took them out first.

Petits farcis became a summer standard for us. I made them hot for dinner or lunch, or I packed them to eat at room temperature for picnics at Quinson, Bauduen, or Esparron, the lakes where we went swimming almost every day after working on the house or going to the markets. When we did our own version of potluck with Adele and Pascal, which we did frequently, Pascal cooked the main dish, and I brought a first course, like *petits farcis*.

GYPSY FÊTE AT SAINTES MARIES DE LA MER

For centuries, gypsies from all over Europe have been making an annual pilgrimage to Saintes-Maries-de-la-Mer in the Camargue region of the Rhone River Delta. They come by the thousands, on May 24 and May 25, to join together in a celebration of their patron saint, Sarah, which culminates in her statue being carried from the church into the sea.

As with many of the ancient rites and fêtes of Provence, legends surround the pilgrimage. The name of the village comes from two Biblical Marys—Mary Jacob, sister of the Virgin Mary, and Mary Salome, mother of apostles John and James. Legend says they were driven out of the Holy Land in a rudderless boat and arrived on the shores of the Rhone River, in what is now Saintes-Maries-de-la-Mer. With them was a young Egyptian girl, their servant Sarah, Mary Magdalene, Martha, and Lazarus, as well as St. Maximinus, and Cedonius the Blind. According to legend, Mary Jacob and Mary Salome stayed in the Camargue, Christianizing the area, and they eventually died there. Mary Magdalene left to live in a cave in the Maure Mountains not far from Marseille. Some legends say she bore Christ's child from whose line sprang the first of the French kings, the Merovingians, whose mythology proclaims that they had come

from the sea. Some of the legends of the Holy Grail even claim that Mary Magdelene's womb was the Holy Grail, carrying Christ's blood with the child, linking it to the legends that the Templar Knights swore to protect, the secret of the Holy Grail.

The gypsies, however, have another version about Sarah, also known as Black Sarah, namely that she did not come by sea from the Holy Land, but was a Princess of the Camargue who saved and sheltered the shipload of refugees from the Holy Land. Over time, Sarah became the patron saint of the gypsies.

As the story goes, after the deaths of the two Marys and Sarah, their remains were buried in a simple chapel in what would become Saintes-Maries-de-la-Mer, or Marys of the Sea. They became the subject of pilgrimages, and in the ninth century, a fortified church was built to hold their remains and to protect them from the Saracens who were invading up the rivers of Europe. In the 1400s, the King of Provence, Roi Rene, had their tombs excavated. Their bones were placed in a casket and a niche was carved out in the high chapel of the church of Notre-Dame-de-la-Mer, where the casket has rested now for more than six hundred years.

One year I went to the gypsy fête with Donald, Ethel, and Oliver. The night we arrived, we walked directly to the overflowing church in the heart of the village. On one side of the church there were gratings and, peering through, we could see into the crypt below where thousands of votive candles were burning. Throngs of people were crowded in front of a statue on a palanquin, both so draped with scarves, dresses, skirts, beads, and flowers that all you could see of the statue was her small black face. A gypsy read Donald's palm.

The next day broke bright and blue and windless. After a quick breakfast, we hurried to the church and were there early enough to get a viewpoint in the square, not too far from the church doors. A dozen or more of the huge, white Camargue horses, with guardiens—the cowboys of the Camargue—astride them, milled around the square, waiting to get into formation to lead the procession to the sea. The women and children were circulating, dressed in the traditional red, white, and black costumes of Arles, lace dripping from high hair combs and sleeves, and their hands lightly tapping on tambourines.

It wasn't long before the guardiens walked the big horses into a double row. The women and children lined up behind them, and the crowd grew quiet. The Sarah emerged on her palanquin, each of its wooden shafts resting on a broad-shouldered gypsy. The men, all wearing white, full-sleeved shirts with tucked fronts and neck scarves of different colors, looked straight ahead, unsmiling. The statue rose three feet in the air above them, even more flower bedecked, jeweled, and robed than we had seen her in the crypt the night before. The horses started to move, the costumed women followed, and behind them came Sarah. From the church emerged more gypsies, and then more poured into the streets from the side. The procession to the sea was underway. Tourists like us, kept pace alongside, cameras clicking.

From the boardwalk, where we stopped, we could see the horses prancing out in the sea, the sunlight glinting in the spray they roused, and their riders holding aloft the streaming banners. The men carrying the statue were nearly waist-high in the water, holding up the statue to be blessed by the gold-and-white robed priest standing in a wooden boat, slightly rocking in the waves.

The following crowd swarmed into the sea as well, joining the horses and gypsies. At that point, I took Oliver and Ethel's hands and headed back into the village, aware that we had witnessed something otherworldly.

Petits Farcis

Serves 6

These are one of the most typical of Provençal dishes. They can be served hot or at room temperature and are perfect for picnics. Use the Provençal round zucchini if you can find them.

4 cups cubed dry bread
3 cups milk
3 red bell peppers
4 small long eggplants
4 round zucchini or 4 small long ones
4 small to medium tomatoes
1½ pounds bulk pork sausage or leftover lamb, finely minced
4 cloves garlic, minced
1 onion, minced
3 medium eggs, beaten
½ cup chopped fresh parsley
¼ minced fresh thyme
2 teaspoons freshly ground black pepper
1 teaspoon sea salt
2 tablespoons olive oil

Put the bread cubes and the milk in a bowl to soak while you prepare the vegetables. If the bread is very hard and stale, it will soak up a lot of milk and take as long as 15 minutes to soften. If it is still somewhat fresh, it will soak up just a little milk in just a few minutes; leaving it longer will make it soggy.

Cut the peppers in half lengthwise and discard the seeds and the ribs. Set aside. Cut the eggplants in half lengthwise. Scoop out the pulp, forming shells ½ inch thick. Put the scooped-out flesh in a mixing bowl. Cut the round zucchini in half crosswise, or if long zucchini, in half lengthwise, and scoop out the pulp, forming shells about ⅓ inch thick. Add the pulp to the bowl holding the eggplant pulp. Set the eggplant and zucchini shells aside.

Cut the tomatoes in half crosswise and scoop out a heaping tablespoon of meat from the center of each half. Put 2 scoops of the tomato in a small bowl to use later. Discard the rest or reserve for another use. Put the tomatoes with the other vegetable shells.

Preheat an oven to 350 degrees F. Finely chop the eggplant and zucchini pulp and return it to the bowl. Squeeze the milk from the bread and then add the bread to the bowl along with the sausage meat, garlic, onion, eggs, parsley, thyme, black pepper, salt, and the reserved tomato pulp. Mix well and then try a small bit of the mixture and taste for seasoning. If it tastes too bland, add more salt and pepper.

Rub the vegetable shells gently with the olive oil and then fill each of them with some of the sausage mixture. The stuffing should mound slightly in the shells, as it will shrink as it cooks. Place the stuffed vegetables on a large, ungreased baking sheet and bake in the preheated oven until the meat is browned and cooked through and the vegetable shells are tender but not collapsing, about 35 to 45 minutes.

Serve hot or at room temperature.

Savory Bread Pudding Layered with Asparagus, Fontina, and Mixed Spring Herbs

Serves 6 to 8

Save up your leftover bread for a week or so, especially the ends and slices from baguettes and any pieces of specialty breads such as focaccia. Let them get good and dry, even hard, so they will absorb the milk. Heavy, chewy breads make a dense pudding; lighter breads result in a softer, puddinglike texture. Served with slices of smoky ham or grilled salmon fillets, this pudding is a good late breakfast or brunch dish.

12 to 16 thick slices dry baguette or country bread
2½ to 3 cups milk
1 pound asparagus
5 eggs
1 teaspoon sea salt
1 teaspoon freshly ground black pepper
¼ cup freshly grated Romano cheese
4 ounces Fontina cheese, grated
4 ounces Gruyére cheese, grated
½ cup chopped, mixed fresh herbs, such as chives, parsley, and tarragon or sage,
    thyme, and marjoram
1 tablespoon butter, cut into small bits

Place the bread in a single layer in a shallow dish. Pour 2½ cups milk over the top. Let soak until the bread has absorbed the milk and becomes soft, about 30 minutes. Press the bread slices to extract the milk. Measure the milk; you should have ½ cup milk left after squeezing. If not, set aside the additional ½ cup milk, and the bread, for use later.

While the bread is soaking, trim the asparagus, removing the woody ends. Cut the stalks on the diagonal into thin slivers each about 2 inches long and ⅜ inch thick. Arrange the slivered asparagus on a steamer rack and place over gently boiling water. Cover and steam until barely tender, 2 or 3 minutes. Immediately place the asparagus under cold running water until cold. Drain and set aside.

Preheat an oven to 350 degrees F. Butter a 3-quart mold—a soufflé dish works well.

In a bowl, beat together the eggs, salt, pepper, and the ½ cup milk until well blended. Layer one-third of the bread in the prepared dish. Set 6 to 8 asparagus slivers aside and top the bread layer with half of the remaining asparagus and half of the mixed herbs. Strew one-third of each of the cheeses over the asparagus. Repeat the layers, using half of the remaining bread, all of the remaining asparagus and herbs, and half of the remaining cheese. Arrange the remaining bread on top, strew the remaining cheese over it, and garnish with the reserved asparagus slivers. Pour the milk-egg mixture over the layers and then dot with the butter.

Bake in the preheated oven until the top is crusty brown and a knife inserted in the middle of the pudding comes out clean, about 45 minutes.

Walnut, Black Olive, and Dried Tomato Tapenade

Serves 4

This is a rich, earthy spread but also a healthy one. The amount of oil you will need to purée the mixture to a spreadable consistency will depend upon how much oil is in the olives and the tomatoes.

⅓ cup pitted black olives
⅓ cup walnuts
¼ cup oil-packed dried tomatoes
1 teaspoon fresh thyme leaves
Extra-virgin olive oil as needed

Start by chopping one-third cup of pitted black olives. Do the same with an equal amount of walnuts. Coarsely chop one-quarter cup of olive-oil-packed dried tomatoes. Put the olives, walnuts, and tomatoes in a food processor along with ½ teaspoon of the tomato oil, and the thyme leaves and process until all is well mixed.

Slowly add extra-virgin olive oil, processing until the mixture reaches the desired consistency for spreading. You will have about 1 cup of tapenade.

Dandelion Salad

Serves 4

From late fall through early spring, the saw-toothed leaves of dandelions start poking up around the edges of vineyards, orchards, roadsides, and creeks. They are at their mildest when harvested before the appearance of the characteristic yellow flower. Walking in the countryside and collecting dandelions for lunch or dinner is a fine way to spend a morning or afternoon.

4 cups wild dandelion greens and their roots, or cultivated dandelion greens
    mixed with baby spinach
1 teaspoon crushed garlic, minced
½ cup extra-virgin olive oil
3 tablespoons red wine vinegar
½ teaspoon sea salt
1 teaspoon freshly cracked black pepper
2 ounces roulade (pancetta) or thick-cut bacon, cut into pieces
    1 inch long and ½ inch wide (about ¼ cup)
2 hard-cooked eggs, finely chopped
2 tablespoons minced red onion

Rinse and clean the greens carefully, discarding any old or bruised leaves. If using wild dandelion greens, trim and use the root as well. Dry the greens well in a salad spinner or with a towel and set aside.

In a small bowl, stir the garlic into the olive oil and then stir in the vinegar, salt, and pepper to form a vinaigrette. In a small skillet, cook the roulade or bacon over medium heat until just crisp, 3 to 5 minutes. Using a slotted spoon, remove to paper towels to drain.

Put the vinaigrette in a large bowl. Add the greens, turning them gently with two spoons until well coated. Top with the chopped eggs, bacon, and onion. Serve at once.

A Wedding to Remember

Late one summer afternoon, I returned to Provence for a special occasion. When I drove up the familiar winding road to my house, I could see a dozen or more cars parked helter-skelter across the road near the Lamys' house. It was going to be a big family wedding, held two days hence, with all the extended members in attendance. Robert and Françoise Lamy, each almost eighty, were beginning to slow down a bit, and I suspected this might be the last big, intact family event. Instead of putting on the wedding feast at the family home, as for previous weddings, this one would be at the salle des fêtes, for close friends and family, with the ritual post-ceremony apéritif for most of the village being held at their home beforehand.

I opened up the house, turning the heavy key in the lock of the front door, and went directly into the kitchen. A bowl of peaches was on the table with a note from Françoise under it, inviting me to dinner at seven. I ate one of the juicy peaches, made myself a cup of coffee, and then went upstairs and unpacked.

At seven, someone, probably one of the grandchildren, rang the big brass gong the Lamys use to call large groups of family to meals. A minute later, when I walked across the road, more than two dozen people were collected around and under the four spreading mulberry trees that shaded the vast flagstone terrace. Robert and his sons were pouring apéritifs, offering pastis, vin d'orange, or kir, while several of the younger granddaughters were passing bowls of nuts and olives, in between eating them. Long tables covered in an assortment of cloths were set in an "L" shape.

The younger grandchildren brought the first course to the tables, big bowls of sliced tomatoes from the garden, mixed with tuna, chopped eggs, and red onion, and dressed with lots of olive oil, salt, and pepper. Robert doesn't like vinegar, so it was absent. We all had at least two helpings, sopping up the juices with the abundant bread, cleaning our plates for the main dish, which was rice with ratatouille made from eggplants, peppers, zucchini, tomatoes, and basil from the garden just on the other side of the terrace where we were eating.

We sat until late under the mulberries, as we always do, sipping our wine and finishing our cheese and fruit. The younger children had cleared the table and started the dishwasher and were now off in their own world.

The moon, nearly full, illuminated the wheat fields and vineyards around us as we sat talking about the next day. More extended family on both sides were arriving, some in the morning, others later.

"So, we'll need to prepare lunch and dinner tomorrow—we'll be around thirty. We also need to fill and cook the tarts and make the tapenade and anchoïade for the wedding apéritif party. We'll be about 120 people for the apéritif, and we've already made the eight hundred tart shells we need," said Delphine, the eldest granddaughter, twenty-eight, who was in charge of the apéritif foods. Like her brother, she had spent part of a summer with me, and she and I had shared many

food adventures in both California and France, including cooking live lobsters, digging potatoes, and planting vegetable gardens.

"It's our last day to prepare, because the day after we have to be at the mairie at eleven," she announced.

Marriage, by law a civil ceremony in France and the only legally valid one, takes place at the mairie, the city hall, which sometimes has a specifically designated salle de marriage. A religious ceremony is an option but has no legal status in the eyes of the state. The civil ceremony is not unlike being in court, but the attendees are better dressed and generally include only the most immediate family, or intimate friends, depending on the size of the city hall and whether or not there will be a church ceremony as well. Donald and I had been married at the salle de marriage at the mairie in Aix-en-Provence, but that was a much larger setting than a village city hall.

The next morning, after a jet-lagged sleep behind my shuttered windows in the deep silence of the countryside, I went across the road to help. It was 9:30, and the tables under the mulberries held the remains of morning café au lait, bread, butter, jam, and cereal bowls. These were quickly cleared, and cutting boards and knives set out. Dinner that night was to be a big couscous.

"We'll finish all the cooking this morning, then this afternoon we're going down to the community center to decorate," Delphine told me after the morning round of kisses. Then it was time to get to work on the couscous.

"Georgeanne, toi, tu coupe les carottes. Tatie, tu coupe les cour-gettes." She gave us each a task—chopping the onions, garlic, carrots, zucchini, and green beans—while she prepared the restaurant-size pot of chicken and the broth, adding local garbanzo beans that Françoise had purchased the previous fall. As we finished chopping the vegetables, she added those.

Françoise's kitchen easily held the six of us around the long wooden table that served for both working and eating. The kitchen had been modernized several times, but the glossy, dark red tiles on the long counter holding the sink, dishwasher, and cooktop remain. The wall behind the counter, red tiles as well, is fitted with two built-in ovens. Above them is a shelf where she keeps a collection of old Provençal terra-cotta cookware. Best of all, the kitchen has a generous, thigh-low window that opens on the terrace. Light pours into the kitchen, and Françoise sets her flats of vegetables and fruits from the garden on the sill, working out of them as she cooks.

That morning, the kitchen quickly gave up its smell of morning coffee to that of chicken and herbs, and by eleven the broth for the couscous, rich with vegetables and tender chicken, was gently bubbling on the stove. All that remained was to cook the couscous itself that evening, just before serving, and for the men to grill the merguez sausages that would be part of the dish.

Delphine and her designated crew of cousins, clad in shorts and bathing suits, had been diligently at work in the dining room, forming an assembly line circling the large round pear-wood table, which was covered in plastic to protect it. They were filling bite-size tarts with various fillings, then storing the cooked tarts in boxes as they laughed and chatted. Delphine had made a classic quiche filling with a savory custard and Gruyére cheese and another with creamed spinach; the crew spooned the fillings directly into the partially baked shells. Some of the shells were spread first with mustard before being filled and topped with slices of cherry tomatoes.

"Oh, that one was my mother's idea. The mustard flavors the custard without being mixed into it. We're making big tarts for lunch today, with the same filling as the little tarts, so you can taste everything then. Here, can you start filling the lunch tarts?" She indicated a stack of eight tart tins, each with a lightly golden, partially baked shell.

"Make three of the tomato—I know everyone likes those, and I bet you will, too."

FÊTE COMPAGNARDE

Country feasts appear all over Provence, often as part of a celebration or fête. The notices are posted on flyers nailed on telephone poles and taped on the windows of local bakeries, bar-tabacs, and city halls. They might be advertised as a *Repas Compagnard* or *Repas Champêtre*. *Champêtre* is rather an old-fashioned term, which harks back to earlier times, while *campagnard* is more commonly used today. Both refer to something related to the country.

Whatever the name, the style of the feast is usually long tables set out in a village square, in an orchard, or in a wheat field and covered with white butcher paper, where a simple meal is served, with lots of wine and bread. You might find such a *repas* with grilled meats, salads, and desserts; another with soupe au pistou as the featured main dish; and another, if you're by the sea, with platters of sardines as the centerpiece.

The meal is made with whatever is local and regional, so you'll find the food varies from place to place, which is part of the attraction.

Fêtes Compagnardes are also a cherished style for private celebrations like weddings and anniversaries. I attended my first when one of my neighbors' sons got married. It began with the wedding

ceremony at the village church perched high on a hill. The newly married couple, he in tails and top hat, she in a floating pouf of a white gown with a veil held on by a wreath of flowers, was helped into the back of a pickup truck festooned with ribbons and flowers—a modern-day version of the traditional Provençal wedding cart. As we tossed rice at them, the truck wound down the twisting road to the home of the groom's parents, across the road from mine.

Tables were set out on the lawn, dressed with white linen and small bouquets of fresh lavender and herbs, and they edged almost into the fields and orchards beyond. Punch was ladled out to us in glass cups; toasts with tapenade and other spreads—along with olives, and savory pastries—were delivered to the tables by the youngest family members.

To be honest, I don't remember the exact meal that night, just how happy everyone was. There was lots of music and dancing, champagne and wine, and a tiered wedding cake. However, at other fête de campagnarde weddings and anniversaries, I've been served such dishes as salade Niçoise, grilled leg of lamb, platters of grilled pork chops and sausages, cheeses, and even small fruit tarts in addition to the wedding cake.

My friend, Joanne, and I—with Donald and her husband Guild—put on our own fête campagnarde one summer at their house in Provence. We spitted and stuffed a lamb, then grilled it for hours over oak coals, turning it on the spit, and basting it with bundled branches of fresh rosemary dipped in garlic-laden olive oil, until the lamb was golden brown outside but still rose-rare inside. We carved it on a large board set over trestles and served platters of the meats and the vegetable rice stuffing to our guests, neighbors mostly, who numbered about fifteen. Sometimes you'll find village feasts featuring the same meal—it's called a michoui, a North African tradition that has become popular in France.

Here at our house in the country in northern California my husband and I have had many campagnard style feasts, including three weddings. The largest, for 250 guests, was for the wedding of my daughter, Ethel. Tables were spread out across the open spaces under the ancient black walnut tree and as far as the grape arbor that borders the fields. For the tables, bouquets were made of roses and sunflowers cut short to fit into glass jars. Sparkling lights were strung in the trees and among the grapes. The meal was simple. After the champagne apéritif, people drifted toward their seats. The tables were set with wine bottles and fresh baguettes, and buffet tables held platters of heirloom tomato salad, a Mesclun salad, and one of yellow and green beans. A huge grill turned out lamb and halibut skewers along with eggplants, peppers, onions, beets, and Belgian endive, and these were served on platters as well. The wedding cake was multitiered and covered with chocolate ganache. The grand finale, after the cake and champagne toasts and the dancing, was French onion soup served around midnight for the fifty or so remaining guests.

If you come across a fête campagnarde in Provence, I highly recommend you subscribe, and I would also encourage you to host your own, wherever you live. The food is simple and the conviviality irrepressible.

Wedding Tart (Tomato Tart)

Serves 6

This is the tart I helped Delphine and the others make for the Lamy wedding. Like everyone else I know in France, Delphine and her crew chose to use ready-to-roll fresh pie dough, readily available everywhere.

1 ready-to-roll fresh pie dough
2 tablespoons Dijon mustard
2 cups sliced tomatoes (or enough to cover the tart pan in a single layer)
⅛ cup extra-virgin olive oil
Sprinkling fine sea salt
Sprinkling freshly ground pepper
Sprinkling fresh thyme
1 cup Gruyére cheese, grated

Preheat an oven to 400 degrees F. Roll out the dough on a floured surface until it is about 14 inches in diameter, just the size to fit a 12-inch tart pan with a removable bottom. Pat the dough into the bottom and up the sides of the pan and trim the edges even with the rim.

Now, here is Delphine's trick. Spread the bottom of the tart with a thin layer of Dijon mustard. Cover this with a tightly packed, single layer of sliced tomatoes. Sprinkle them with the olive oil, sea salt, black pepper, and thyme. Finish with a layer of Gruyére cheese. Place in the oven and bake the tart until the crust is golden and pulling away slightly from the rim of the pan and the top is very lightly browned, about 20 to 25 minutes. Remove the tart to a rack to cool for at least 20 minutes and up to an hour. Slice into wedges to serve.

Squash Blossom Rice

Serves 6

Squash blossoms as well as the squashes themselves are used in cooking in Haute Provence. Frequently the blossoms are stuffed with an herbed soft cheese, or with a mixture of minced and seasoned meat, often lamb. The stuffed blossoms are then sautéed or baked and served with a sauce, usually a light tomato sauce. Here the preparation is simpler but still benefits from the striking color and "green" squash flavor of the blossoms.

In the garden, the squash blossoms open wide after dawn, then close by midmorning. It is best to pick them when fully opened, and they are sold that way in the outdoor markets. Should you have a closed blossom, however, it can be opened by plunging it for a minute or two in ice water. Do check inside the blossoms for trapped insects.

1½ tablespoons unsalted butter
1½ tablespoons extra-virgin olive oil
⅓ cup minced shallots
1½ cups long-grain white rice
10 squash blossoms
1½ cups water
1½ cups chicken broth
1 teaspoon freshly ground black pepper
½ teaspoon sea salt

In a saucepan, melt the butter with the olive oil over medium heat. When the mixture is foamy, add the shallot and sauté until translucent, 2 or 3 minutes. Add the rice and cook, stirring, until it begins to change color, just a minute or two. Stir in the squash blossoms, and then add the water, chicken broth, pepper, and salt. Raise the heat to high and bring to a boil. Reduce the heat to low, cover, and simmer until the rice is tender, about 20 minutes.

Remove to a warmed serving bowl and serve at once.

Late Summer Pears Poached in Young Wine

Serves 6 to 8

For me, this is a perfect fall dessert. It combines sunny memories of summer with the promise of cozy fireside winter days. A young, slightly rough wine like a Cahors from southwest France is perfect for the poaching, but a similar California wine is equally good.

Look for pears that ripen late in the season, such as Boscs or Red Bartletts. These are good choices because they are generally firmer than the earlier ripening varieties and will hold their shape during poaching.

Heavy cream mixed with rosemary and a tiny bit of freshly ground black pepper accentuates the flavor of the wine-poached pears.

4 pears
½ bottle red wine
1½ tablespoons sugar
½ cup heavy cream
2 tablespoons finely chopped fresh rosemary

Halve the pears lengthwise, leaving the stem intact on one half. Scoop out and discard the seeds. Remove the string that runs down the center from the stem end to the seed cavity. You may peel the pears or leave them unpeeled. I think keeping the golden green skin on half of the pears and peeling the skins from the remaining halves makes a pretty presentation.

In a skillet or saucepan large enough to hold all the pear halves in a single layer, bring the wine and 1 tablespoon of the sugar to a boil, stirring to dissolve the sugar. Cook over high heat for 3 to 4 minutes. Reduce the heat, add the pears, and poach until just tender, 15 to 20 minutes. Do not overcook the pears, or they will become mushy.

Transfer the pears and the poaching liquid to a glass or ceramic bowl and let stand for several hours at room temperature. Turn the pears from time to time. They will become a beautiful, deep garnet color as they absorb the wine.

In a small bowl, mix the cream, the remaining 1 tablespoon of sugar, and the rosemary. To serve the pears, put a few spoonfuls of the cream mixture onto each dessert plate. Add a pear half and a single spoonful of the poaching liquid.

An Extended Family

After an hour or so, the guests began to drift away, except for those of us invited to the *fête de marriage* at the community center. I drove down on my own, suspecting I might want to leave earlier than some of my compatriots. I arrived about the same time as everyone else, about sixty-five of us, and Marie grabbed my arm, saying, "Let's sit together."

I shared a table with Marie and Marcel and an assortment of Lamy relatives, including Robert's brother and sister, feeling more than ever a part of the family.

Platters of smoked salmon, pâté in puff pastry, *cornichons*, thin slices of salt-cured ham, almonds, and olives had been set on all the tables, and we served ourselves the first course, passing the platters among us, commenting on the wedding, how happy Laurent looked, and how good the wine was.

When the first course was finished, Marie and I got up and went back to the kitchen to help the caterers, friends of ours from the village. We arranged thin slices of cold beef tenderloin on one set of trays, thin slices of cold pork on another, garnishing all with quartered tomatoes and sprigs of basil from Françoise's garden. Then we brought the trays out to buffet tables already groaning with bowls of roasted red peppers and eggplants, tomato and mozzarella salad, potato salad, and green salad, all liberally dressed in olive oil.

As I lay in bed that night, snug in a bedroom familiar to me for half my life, looking at the ceiling of hand-hewn planks and the smooth, plastered walls lined with bookshelves, I thought how lucky I was to have such a life: one in California, another here. In just six weeks I'd be back in California, bags loaded, to teach another series of cooking classes. But first I'd spend time in Provence picking tomatoes and melons and cooking with Marie and Françoise and enjoying long, leisurely meals with all my friends who had become my extended family.

A Kitchen Full of Memories

In the twilight of the vaulted room, the fireplace looms, promising warmth and companionship on this October evening. I've built a fire of oak and pine deep in the hearth, and when the wood is burnt down to glowing chunks, I'll put on a handful or two of grape prunings and grill my lamb chops. They're sitting on a plate in the kitchen, rubbed with olive oil and sprinkled with wild thyme. I've already been to the garden to pick young frisée, arugula, and thick stalks of white-ribbed chard. The greens are washed now, sitting in the enameled colander, a wedding present I brought here long ago from California. A fresh goat cheese, like the ones I used to make, is resting in the refrigerator. Soon I'll broil it to put on top of my salad.

I pour myself a glass of rosé and sip it while I cook the chard and make a béchamel sauce. I put out a few olives, black and green, in a little bowl I bought at the market the previous year. It's pale yellow, and I like the way the olives look in it.

The chard, mixed with the béchamel and topped with bread crumbs and butter, is baking, so I set the wooden table in front of the fireplace with my favorite antique French napkins, huge, heavily embroidered squares that once were part of someone's trousseau. One, folded in half, serves as a place mat, the other as it was intended. I open the glass-fronted armoire and bring out two brown-rimmed, mustard-gold plates, part of the set Marie gave me as a housewarming gift when electricity and plumbing were finally installed. An antique silver knife and fork from a flea market finish the table setting, along with a water glass, a pitcher, and a terra-cotta dish to hold the wine bottle. I'll bring the small bowls of sea salt and pepper later, bowls like the one the olives are in. A small glass vase set in the middle of the table holds the red and golden grape leaves I picked earlier from the vineyard that borders the garden.

The aroma of the gratin tells me it's almost ready. The timing is perfect. The coals are glowing, ready to cook the lamb. My grill consists of a long-legged wrought-iron trivet I inherited with the house, on which I put a grilling rack, set over the hottest part of the coals. The lamb sizzles when I set it on the grill, and I can already taste the promise of crisp bits of fat and the rosy meat infused with the fragrance of the thyme. I pour a little more wine while I tend the chops, turning them several times. Just before the chops are ready, I broil the cheese.

As soon as the chops are done, I move them to a plate set on the hearth. They'll rest and stay warm while I have my salad, dressed with olive oil from Robert Lamy's brother and my homemade vinegar, topped with the broiled goat cheese.

Sitting down to my salad, I look through the window and see the sky has turned deep violet, announcing the dark and the silence to come. I've never been anywhere as quiet as my house in Provence, set deep in the countryside amid small patches of vineyards and wheat carved out of the surrounding forests of oak, pine, and juniper.

The cheese is hot, slightly runny at the edges where it blends with the vinaigrette and catches the leaves of frisée and arugula. I finish the last bit on my plate, cleaning it with a piece of baguette and a deep sigh of contentment.

Mustard-Glazed Spring Carrots with Sage Lamb Chops

Serves 4

As soon as the first carrots of spring are as big as my finger, I begin harvesting them. Small, delicate carrots are very tender and taste quite different from large carrots or those that have been topped and kept in storage. In the market, you can readily spot freshly dug carrots because they still have their leafy green tops.

Before being glazed with a honey-mustard sauce, the carrots are steamed with half an inch or so of their green tops left on. The lamb chops are cooked atop a very thin bed of salt and fresh sage leaves in a very hot frying pan.

¼ cup honey mustard
1 tablespoon butter
Juice of 1 lemon
½ teaspoon sea salt
12 to 16 small carrots, tops intact, 6 to 8 inches long
20 to 30 fresh sage leaves
4 lamb shoulder chops, about ½ inch thick
½ teaspoon freshly ground black pepper
½ cup water

In a saucepan large enough to hold the carrots, combine the mustard, butter, lemon juice, and a pinch of the salt. Cook over low heat until the butter melts and the mixture is thick enough to coat the back of a spoon, 10 to 15 minutes.

Trim the green tops from the carrots to within ½ inch of the crown. Arrange the carrots on a steamer rack over gently boiling water. Cover and steam until tender, 5 or 6 minutes.

Remove the carrots from the steamer and put them in the saucepan with the mustard sauce. Turn the carrots to coat each one completely with the sauce. Simmer the carrots over the lowest heat while you cook the chops.

In a frying pan large enough to hold all the chops at one time, sprinkle the remaining salt and all of the sage leaves. Heat the frying pan over high heat until the edges of the sage leaves begin to curl, about 2 minutes. Add the chops and sear them over high heat for 2 or 3 minutes on each side. Sprinkle with the pepper and then add the water and reduce the heat to low. Cover the pan and simmer for 5 minutes.

Put a lamb chop on each plate; be sure to include a few sage leaves and a spoonful of pan juices. Arrange 3 or 4 carrots in a fan next to each plate and serve.

Sage Roasted New Potatoes

Serves 4

In this easy-to-prepare recipe, new potatoes are first rubbed with olive oil, salt, and pepper, and then roasted with whole sage clusters. Their skins become crispy, while their centers turn soft and creamy. This contrast in texture, together with the fragrance and flavor of just-harvested sage, makes this an exceptional dish.

12 to 15 new potatoes, each about 1½ inch in diameter
¼ cup olive oil
1 teaspoon sea salt
2 teaspoons freshly ground black pepper
10 to 12 clusters fresh sage

Preheat an oven to 350 degrees F. Rub the potatoes with the olive oil, salt, pepper, and 2 of the sage clusters. Put the potatoes and all the sage clusters in an attractive ovenproof dish just large enough to hold them in a single layer. Bake until the potato skins are crispy and the centers are tender when pierced, about I hour.

EPILOGUE

As I read and reflect upon the story told here, my story, first written more than ten years ago, I am surprised by both how little has changed and how much has changed. Esparron-sur-Verdon, where Donald and I bought our first goats, is now a bustling, tourist-packed destination for vacationers from all over Europe. The rocky outcroppings above the lake and the foot of the village where we parked when we sought out the goats are now a gated, metered parking area. New villas sweep up the hills behind the small, old village where somewhere among the beach ball and candy shops, cafes and postcard kiosks, is the barn where Madam kept her herd of goats. I looked for it recently, but found nothing that I could say with certainty was where the narrative of my life in rural France had begun.

Climbing over the hill, past the villas and into the ever-present pine and oak forest to descend the other side and cross the river, a matter of only a few kilometers of twisting road, is to arrive at Saint-Martin-de-Brömes, where Ethel and her French husband and children have a little house in the village, where they come in the summers. Ethel now takes her children to the lake in Esparron where we took her and her brother for picnics and swimming.

The transhumance, which was beginning to fade from practice and memory when I met the Audibert brothers, is now in full resurgence. An increasing number of young men and women are going to school to become shepherds, there are once again fêtes in the villages celebrating the passage of the sheep on their way to the high mountains in June, and again in September when they return to the valleys. I can hear their bells from my bedroom window as the grand *troupeaux* pass through the narrow valley below my house, continuing the ancient movement of animals, directed by the rhythm of the seasons.

There are more supermarkets, and new bio or organic and natural food stores are appearing in all the villages, but the open markets continue, just as they have for centuries. They are more crowded and bustling than ever before, especially in the summers when the villages are packed with visitors stocking up for their holidays, filling the nearby cafes and restaurants, and soaking up the sun. Many of the vendors I've known over the years are still there, selling their chickens, cheese, cabbages, and tomatoes, just like I used to do. I never tire of going to the markets and wandering among the stalls, overloading my basket as always because everything looks so beautiful and fresh and irresistible.

The greatest changes are in the people. My beloved neighbors and friends, Marcel Palazolli and Françoise Lamy, have passed away, along with M. Bruno and one of the handsome masons who served the apéritifs at the bouillabaisse party. Toddlers, like mine, have grown into adults with children of their own. Denys and Georgette Fine continue to thrive in spite of their age, now in their eighties, as does Marie Palazolli, who can still be seen every morning and evening cultivating her fruit trees and vast vegetable plots. Donald, with whom I began the great adventure in Provence, died recently, and as I sat with him toward the end, he said, "What a life we had."

I continue on with my life in Provence and in California, cooking, writing, and like Marie, cultivating my garden. I spend as much time as possible with my friends and my family, more often than not around a table sharing good food, wine, and conversation.

The End, For Now

Acknowledgments

Thank you to my publisher, Lisa McGuinness, of Yellow Pear Press, who first had the vision for this book and then enlisted me with her enthusiasm and support. Of course, none of this book would be possible without the magic of Provence and its people, and especially my friends and neighbors there, who have been part of my life since I was in my twenties. It is my second home, and they are my second family.

With my first husband, Donald Brennan, I began a life in Provence that turned into a journey. I remain forever grateful for those shared years and extraordinary times with each other and our children, when life was both fraught with fears and buoyed by hopes.

Many people have come together to make this book a reality. In addition to the early family photos that appear in *My Culinary Journey*, photographers Sara Remington, Natasha McGuinness, and Rose Wright all brought to life the images from my early days. Rose Wright's clean, yet romantic, gorgeous design brought the essence of Provence and my stories to these pages. Copyeditor Kim Carpenter's keen eye was much appreciated, as was proofreader Amy Bauman's attention to detail. A book is always the result of the effort, creativity, and dedication of a team of people.

Thanks, above all, to my husband of thirty years, Jim Schrupp, who is my best friend and biggest supporter and fan and who has shared the latter part of my life in Provence and in California. He is also my personal in-house editor, not to mention that he happily eats everything I cook and occasionally takes over himself.

List of Recipes

Index

About the Aurhor

Georgeanne Brennan is an award-winning cookbook author, journalist, educator and entrepreneur who is nationally recognized for her work. Her expertise ranges from farming and agriculture to history and food lore. She is the recipient of many awards including a James Beard Foundation Award.

In 2014 she launched her online store, La Vie Rustic—Sustainable Living in the French Style, lavierustic.com, which reflects her long-time love affair with France and especially Provence, where she has a home.

In addition to her books Brennan writes regular features for the *San Francisco Chronicle* newspaper's food section and has contributed to *Fine Cooking, Bon Appétit, Cooking Pleasures*, the *New York Times, Garden Design, Metropolitan Home, Horticulture*, and *Organic Gardening*, and is a regular contributor and columnist for *Edible Marin* and *Wine Country*. She has been featured in *Food and Wine, Gourmet*, and *Sunset Magazines*, among others and has appeared on Oprah.com, Good Morning America, and other shows. She lives in Winters, CA, and Provence.

The end for now.